CW01045952

EDITED BY SHEILA HALES

REAL LIVES, REAL TIMES

A NEW WINDMILL BOOK OF NON-FICTION

Heinemann
New Windmills

Heinemann Educational Publishers
Halley Court, Jordan Hill, Oxford OX2 8EJ
A division of Reed Educational and Professional Publishing Ltd

OXFORD MADRID ATHENS FLORENCE
PRAGUE CHICAGO PORTSMOUTH NH (USA)
MEXICO CITY SÃO PAULO SINGAPORE
KUALA LUMPUR TOKYO MELBOURNE
AUCKLAND NAIROBI KAMPALA
IBADAN GABORONE JOHANNESBURG

02 01 00 99 98
10 9 8 7 6 5 4 3 2

ISBN 0 435 12494 3

Cover by Johnathan Satchell
Cover design by The Point
Typeset by 🠶 Tek-Art, Croydon, Surrey
Printed and bound in the United Kingdom by Clays Ltd,
St Ives plc

Contents

Introduction for Teachers

Some time ago I began searching for an anthology of non-fiction texts that I could use with my Key Stage 3 pupils. For a long while there seemed to be very little material available, and then one or two anthologies appeared on the market. These new publications were aimed mainly at Key Stage 4 pupils or the top end of Key Stage 3. I was looking for texts that I could use with *all* Key Stage 3 pupils, and especially Years 7 and 8.

During this time I had put together my own collection of non-fiction texts for use with my younger pupils, and had developed a range of tasks to open up and explore those texts. This work eventually formed the basis of this present anthology, although I have since updated both the selection of texts and the nature of the activities.

Meeting Curriculum Requirements

Real Lives, Real Times has been designed to meet the requirement of the English National Curriculum to:

• Introduce pupils to 'a range of non-fiction texts'.

The tasks are devised to provide opportunities whereby pupils may:

• 'Select information'
• 'Compare and synthesize information drawn from different texts'
• 'Make effective use of information in their own work'
• 'Evaluate how information is presented'.

(English in the National Curriculum, January 1995)

Thematic Sections With Differentiation

The texts are organized into thematic sections. I have found that most Key Stage 3 pupils prefer to work within a theme, and that they enjoy the challenge of comparing texts. Each section contains a mixture of non-fiction extracts which are arranged in ascending order of difficulty. You may choose to tackle all the material within one section, or you may wish to differentiate between texts according to the range of ability within your class.

The activities are targeted to allow for a range of reading and writing responses, and are also differentiated to relate to the level of reading difficulty which the texts present. Because the extracts vary in length and difficulty, they provide opportunities for group reading.

Progression

The sections are arranged in ascending order of difficulty so that easier sections are grouped in the first half of the book, and the more difficult ones in the second. Certainly the final section, 'First World War', provides the most challenging material for more able pupils. However, I have found that even pupils in Year 7 who 'struggle' with reading were fascinated by the content of these texts when they heard them read aloud.

Non-fiction texts often appeal to a large majority of pupils once they understand that they are reading about real people and true events. I hope, therefore, that you will find this book a valuable resource to help you to develop all your pupils as effective and enthusiastic readers.

Sheila Hales

Introduction for Students

The book that you are about to read contains a broad selection of non-fiction texts. Unlike fiction texts, which are made-up stories, non-fiction texts claim to be true. In this book you will meet real people, in real situations, solving real problems. You will also discover a lot of interesting facts and information.

I've tried to include many different examples of non-fiction; so whether you prefer to read letters or diaries, advertisements or newspaper articles, I'm sure that you will find something to fascinate or astonish you.

The activities are there to help you to understand the texts, and the way they work. Some activities ask you to look closely at the texts; others ask you to create your own pieces of non-fiction writing.

As well as helping you to understand non-fiction, I hope that the book will also give you a great deal of pleasure. Reading non-fiction is a way of peeping into other people's lives and discovering their secret hopes, fears and dreams. Non-fiction texts tell us about the world we live in, and about other times and other places. And the best non-fiction texts help us to understand a little more about ourselves.

Happy reading.

Sheila Hales

Section 1
Children's Authors

What makes authors write, and where do they get their ideas for stories and books? How do authors create characters and plots, and what sort of problems do they face during the process of writing? The extracts in this first section will help you to find out about a few well-known children's authors.

Read the introductions and extracts which follow before working through the activities on pages 15–16.

Extract 1: How I Created . . . Paddington Bear (page 3)

Michael Bond is the creator of the Paddington Bear stories. In this article, which appeared in the *Radio Times*, he talks about how the idea for his character originated and developed. Although the stories are aimed at very young children, the article is written for adults to read.

Extract 2: The Spying Game (page 5)

Robert Owen is one of four Year 6 and 7 students of Lanesborough School, Guildford, who wrote to *Books For Keeps* about novels that they had enjoyed.

Extract 3: Nigel Hinton Visits Bartholomew School (page 6)

The interview with Nigel Hinton is part of the publicity material produced by Heinemann to encourage children to enjoy the books that they produce.

Extract 4: Gillian Cross, Author (page 9)

The article about Gillian Cross is taken from a BBC book called *Treasure Islands 2*. This is an information book about popular children's writers.

Extract 5: Letter to the Editor (page 13)

Jean Ure has written many books for children and young people; some of her most popular books are *Plague 99*, *A Proper Little Nooryeff* and *Tealeaf On The Roof*. In this letter she is writing to the editor of the magazine *Books For Keeps* to ask for advice about her new book.

Extract 1

HOW I CREATED ...
PADDINGTON BEAR

A last-minute shopping trip to Selfridges one Christmas gave Michael Bond the idea for the bear from darkest Peru.

" He was largely an accident. I had a blank sheet of paper in the typewriter and, unless you put some words on it, blank it stays. I was doodling with words, warming up my mind. I'd written for adults before but never written a story for children and didn't intend to then. But I liked the lines I'd typed. Those few words were joined by other words and became the first Paddington Bear story.

I'd bought my wife a bear the previous year and we'd called that Paddington, though he was nothing like the Paddington everyone knows now. A pleasing name I thought, sort of West Country connotations, reassuring.

It was Christmas Eve 1957, a foul evening, and I was worried that I hadn't bought as much for my wife as I intended. Usual last-minute panic. I went into Selfridges and there was this last, remaining bear on a shelf and I brought him home and he's been with us ever since. Twist of fate. If I'd diligently bought all my presents when I should have done, I'd never have walked into that store, never bought a bear, never written about one.

The now famous Paddington is quite a polite bear. He's like my father who never went out of the house without his hat on in case he met an acquaintance. He was a great hat-doffer.

Paddington is also how I wish I was. The sort of thing I'm talking about is this: we used to live in Haslemere in Surrey and I drove down to the station one morning to find the car park barred and the man from British Rail informing me I couldn't come in. But I could see six or seven empty parking places, so I said "Why can't I?" And the man replied: "Well, if I let you in they'll all want to come in." I meekly drove away, knowing that in two or three weeks' time I'd have thought up a suitable, crushing reply.

Paddington wouldn't have been put off. He'd have demanded a proper explanation and, of course, he has a very hard stare which gets things done.

When I wrote the first story, he came from darkest Africa. My agent pointed out that there are no bears there. I changed it to darkest Peru.

Mr and Mrs Brown whom he lives with are kind people, but they don't know what it's like not to be living in one's own country. It's why Paddington's great friend is Mr Gruber, a refugee. I worked once for the BBC monitoring service which was staffed by many foreign nationals who had fled their countries, so it's a subject I knew something about.

If you ask why Paddington caught on, I think it's because, like all bears, he's comforting. He lives in a world of vandalised phone boxes and all the rest, but he goes back in the evenings to the house in Windsor Gardens, to the safe world I knew as a child. People like that.

99

Michael Bond, *Radio Times*

Extract 2

The Spying Game

A very moving story, about a thirteen-year-old boy's life, just after his father's death. One day he accidentally sees his father's killer, and then, he plans his revenge. First of all he starts with small things, like graffiti on his car and some threatening mail. But after the summer holidays he starts a new school, and he is put in the same class as the killer's son.

I found this book very exciting, and, as I had never read a Pat Moon story before, I did not know what to expect. I thoroughly enjoyed the way that she made me feel that I was there, and my father had been killed. Her sentence beginnings varied considerably and everything was unexpected. I think that one of the only authors around who compares with Pat Moon is Michael Morpurgo. An extract from the book is:

'"What would you rather be," I ask. "Sucked slowly by a python or eaten by a giant spider?"'

This short extract shows that the book has a humorous side to it above the real meaning. I recommend this book to everybody of any age, as the story could really happen to anybody.

Robert Owen, *Books for Keeps*, July 1997

Extract 3

NIGEL HINTON VISITS
Bartholomew School

**Best Selling New Windmill Author Opens Pupils'
Eyes to the Exciting World of Writing**

'Which is your favourite of the books you have written and why?'
ALEXA DOVE

'That's a very tough one. I can't believe that I managed to write them. I suppose I would have to say *Buddy*, not because I like it better than the other books but because a lot happened as a result of it. I wrote the TV script, the second book, *Buddy's Song* which was turned into a movie, I wrote the screen play for the movie and the lyrics for the songs. In fact the album sold so well I received a Gold disk for it. All these things are a result of writing *Buddy*.'

'How long does it take to write a book from the first idea to the finished product?'
CHLOE CORLETT

'That's a difficult one to answer. My first book, *Collision Course* took me about four weeks of writing. Everything since then has taken very much longer. For example, I started thinking about *Buddy's Blues*, the third and final part of the *Buddy* story, when I finished writing *Buddy's Song* which was in 1987, so it has been knocking around inside my head for about eight years. The actual writing time was about nine months of sitting down almost every day and doing some writing. *Buddy* took me fourteen weeks of actual writing but there was a year in which I was writing another version about and eight-year-old boy called Stuart. Stuart eventually became fourteen-year-old Buddy and the story changed quite dramatically – so did it take a year and fourteen weeks, or just fourteen weeks to write? It's difficult to say.'

'Were you good at English when you were at school?'
ADAM PELTAN

'English was probably my best subject at school but I wasn't brilliant at that. I was good but I was never good enough to be top of the class.'

'Did you want to become an author when you were a child and if not, what did you want to be?'
GARY HEWES

'I hadn't the faintest idea what I wanted to be. I never knew what to say when grown-ups asked me so eventually I made something up – I said I wanted to work on a newspaper. I suppose it is something similar to what I do do – write – but I made it up simply to shut them up!'

'Where do you write?'
CATHERINE BALL

'I write in a very small room at the top of my house. You can barely stand up because the roof is so low. In the room are lots of books, a mini hi-fi, loads of CDs, and my guitar. There's also a window but I sit facing the wall because I know that if I were to face the window I'd be looking out all the time!'

New Windmill Book Club Publicity

Extract 4

Gillian Cross, Author

....

'The only way that I can write stories is by imagining that I am one of the people in the story.'

Gillian Cross is a Carnegie Medal winner, an award she won in 1991 for *Wolf*. In 1992 she also won the Whitbread Award and the Smarties Award for *The Great Elephant Chase*. These came after more than ten years of success with such titles as *The Demon Headmaster* and *The Mintyglo Kid*. She was brought up in London, studied English at university and could technically call herself 'Dr Cross', as she has a D.Phil. from Oxford. At one point in her life, she could have become an academic, but just as she was on the verge of taking it up, she made the leap of becoming a children's writer. It came about partly as a result of having children herself. In fact one of her children spurred her into writing the book that many children know her for, *The Demon Headmaster*.

What happened was that her daughter, having read *Save Our School*, was fascinated by the story that one of the characters had written. One bit of it goes like this:

Cracking his whip over the children's heads as they cowered in the corner, the wicked Headmaster smiled ferociously and twirled his moustache. 'You will never escape,' he shouted, 'I've put a bomb somewhere in the school. . .'

Gillian Cross's daughter, Elizabeth, said to her,

'That's much better than the sort of stories you write. Why don't you write a book like that?' And Gillian said, 'I will one day, when I'm not busy, when I'm not writing a great work, I'll write you your book.'

Elizabeth kept on at her about it. She kept saying, 'You haven't written that Headmaster book yet.' Till in the end Gillian Cross knew that she would have to do it. 'When I began to think how you would actually write a book about a wicked Headmaster in a real school, in the sort of school that most people go to, I saw that it couldn't be done simply – because, if my children had terrible troubles with their Headmaster, or their Headteacher, they would come back and tell me and I would stomp in and beat the place up. But there was one way that a Headmaster in a day school could actually do terrible things: that was by hypnotizing all the pupils. The moment I thought of that I could see how the book was going to go. So, to shut Elizabeth up, I wrote it.'

But Gillian Cross's Carnegie Medal winner, *Wolf*, began life in a different way. What she first thought of was what happens at the very beginning of the book where Cassie, the girl, is lying in bed, in the flat, and she hears feet coming along the balcony. The padding feet she had in mind was the sort of atmosphere that one associates with wolves. 'That kind of Red Riding Hood, things-leaping-in-the-night atmosphere.'

'When I was researching it, I went to London Zoo, and I was lucky enough actually to be taken into the enclosure where they keep the wolves. What happened – which I describe in the book and is the only thing I've ever described in my whole life exactly as it happened to me – was that we walked into the middle of the enclosure and the wolves made a circle round us. They moved as if they were working together. One of them sniffed our footsteps, where we'd been. It was very beautiful to see because wolves are very beautiful and it was a perfectly wolfish thing to do. But at the same time, it was the feeling that I would associate with being in a dangerous, urban place; being in a part of a city where I didn't feel very safe. And I knew, because I'd read about wolves, my feelings didn't actually have a great deal to do with real wolves. It was that twin pair of things, those things coming together that really fascinated me all the time I was writing the book.'

He was standing by the window, with his back to her, looking out into the garden. His tracksuit hood was pulled up over his head and he was hunched slightly forward. . .

* 'Lyall – '*

He turned. For a split second her brain froze, putting everything into slow motion. Repeating the same image, over and over again. He turned – and instead of his face there was a senseless, nightmare shape. He turned – and the yellow teeth gnashed suddenly as his jaw snapped open. He turned – and the long grey muzzle flickered at her from every mirror in the room, at a hundred different angles, tinted blue, or pink, or yellow. He turned – Cassie screamed. Wolf!

* The wolf where no wolf should be. Behind the door. Invading the house. Inside the skin of a familiar, trusted person. . . .*

Gillian Cross

....

Favourite Titles

The Great Elephant Chase	Oxford
Wolf	Puffin
The Mintyglo Kid	Mammoth
Chartbreak	Puffin
The Demon Headmaster	Oxford (Eagle)
Save Our School	Mammoth
The Dark Behind the Curtain	Hippo
A Map of Nowhere	Oxford
Roscoe's Leap	Puffin
On The Edge	Puffin

Michael Rosen & Jill Burridge, *Treasure Islands 2*,
BBC Books 1993

Extract 5

 # Letter to the Editor

White Author / Black Characters

Dear Editor

I have a problem. There's a book I am yearning to write and virtually every editor in London has told me that it is not a good idea.

The reason it is not a good idea is that it is about a Black family. And I am White.

These are the standard objections trotted out over and over:

1 You would get a lot of flak.
2 What do you *know* about Black people? (Like, what do you know about little boys or octogenarians or anything else that I don't personally happen to be.)
3 Why do you *want* to write about Black people?
4 Black faces on covers *do not sell books*. (I have no idea whether or not this is true, but it certainly seems to be perceived as true.)

Ultimately, everyone comes back with the same suggestion: 'Why can't you just make them White?' Same story, same characters . . . just a different colour.

If I *could* 'just make them White' I am not at all sure what this would say about the proposed book, since it's a book which would be heavily character- rather than plot-led. And although on the one hand I strongly maintain that the time has come for writers to be able to write about children who are simply *children* – as opposed to White, Black or Asian children – it is nonetheless a fact that within this society the colour of your skin cannot yet, unfortunately, be dismissed as irrelevant.

I have based my family on a real family whom I know – because they happen to live opposite me. I have watched their four girls grow from infancy to young womanhood. Over the years they have become *my* four girls; and the fact that they are Black has inevitably, to a greater or lesser degree, shaped their characters and their destinies. I cannot 'just make them White'.

So . . . am I being unreasonable? Unrealistic? Politically incorrect? Do I just give up and bow to editorial (and economic) pressure, or do I continue the fight?

It would be of enormous value to me to hear the views of my fellow authors and of *BfK* readers in general.

Jean Ure
88 Southbridge Road, Croydon, CR0 1AF

Books for Keeps, July 1997

Activities

1 Re-read the interview with Michael Bond on pages 3–4. Copy and complete the lines below which trace the beginnings of the Paddington Bear stories.

Michael Bond bought his wife ....

....

In the first story ....

....

The writer changed ....

....

Paddington Bear is like ....

.... because ....

Paddington's friend is ....

....

The stories are popular because ....

....

2 Re-read Robert Owen's review of *The Spying Game* on page 5. In pairs, discuss the following questions:
   a How many sentences does Robert use to describe the plot of the novel?

b Why did Robert find the book 'exciting'?

c What does Robert say about sentence beginnings?

d With which other author is Pat Moon compared?

e What does the extract tell the reader about the book?

f Why does Robert recommend the book to 'everybody of any age'?

Think of a book you have really enjoyed. Write a review of the book. Use the questions above as a guide for your own writing.

3 Re-read the questions that the children put to Nigel Hinton, and his answers, from the interview on pages 6–8. Use all the information from the answers to write a profile of the author. You could begin:

Nigel Hinton is now a best-selling author, but when he was young he had no idea . . .

4 Look back at the article about the author, Gillian Cross (pages 9–12). What do you learn about the books, *The Demon Headmaster* and *Wolf*? Write one paragraph, stating which book you would prefer to read, giving reasons for your choice.

5 Do you agree with Jean Ure that she should try to write a book about a Black family? Or, do you agree with the people who say that as Jean Ure is White she should make her characters White? Write a letter to Jean Ure in which you reply to the points she has made, and put forward your own views.

Section 2
Hauntings

People have always been fascinated by seemingly inexplicable events. Often strange noises or sights are attributed to restless spirits. In this section you will read about riverside ghosts, haunted buildings, and the terrifying events that took place at Tedworth.

Read the introductions and extracts which follow before working through the activities on pages 27–28.

Extracts 1 and 2: Chopped Charlie's Last Chance (page 19) and The Terror of Tedworth (page 20)

These two extracts come from one of the 'Horrible Histories' series. These books are written for children, and aim to make history fun (and horrible!)

Extract 3: Haunted by a Fiddler (page 22)

This extract is taken from a book which is *A Guide to Follies and Strange Buildings, Curious Tales and Unusual People*. The book provides a guide to places of interest in Norfolk, Suffolk and Essex.

Extract 4: Haunted Britain – The Real X-Files (page 23)

The next piece of writing about the haunted room at Westwell Hall Private Hotel comes from a magazine devoted to 'true' stories about 'Paranormal, UFOs, Occult, Conspiracies, Ghosts, Aliens, and Weird Science'. How much of the article do *you* believe? Why might the magazine present this article as the truth?

Extract 5: The Walberswick Whisperers (page 24)

The Walberswick Whisperers is taken from a book of supposedly 'true' stories of hauntings on the east coast of Britain. Walberswick is an isolated village in East Anglia. The ferry referred to in the account is a small boat which takes summer visitors from Walberswick, across the River Blyth, to the little town of Southwold.

Extract 6: Diary of Thomas Raikes – 26 December 1832 (page 26)

Thomas Raikes was born in 1777 and died in 1848. He was the friend of some important people of his day, and spent a great deal of money on gambling and keeping up with the latest fashions. He kept a diary from 1831 to 1847, and in the entry on page 26 he describes a strange case of 'second sight'.

Extracts 1 and 2

Chopped Charlie's Last Chance

Charles I was visited by a ghost . . .

The Terror of Tedworth

One of Britain's most famous ghost stories happened in Stuart times. It concerns the *Phantom Drummer of Tedworth*.

Magistrate John Mompasson was visiting the town of Ludgershall in Wiltshire when he heard the deafening sound of a drum.

'What's that horrible racket?' he asked.

'It's a beggar. He has a special licence to beg and to use that drum to attract attention,' his friend explained.

'Look, I know the magistrates round here. None of them would sign a licence like that. Fetch him here.'

So the beggar, William Drury, was brought before Mompasson and showed his licence. It was a very clumsy forgery. Drury went to prison but begged to be allowed to keep the drum. Mompasson refused. Drury escaped from the prison and the drum was sent to Mompasson's house.

For the next two years the house suffered terrible drumming noises. Then the ghost grew more violent . . .

- A bible was burnt.
- An unseen creature gnawed at the walls like a giant rat, purred like a cat and panted like a dog.
- Coins in a man's pocket turned black.
- Great staring eyes appeared in the darkness.
- The spirit attacked the local blacksmith with a pair of tongs.

- A horse died of terror in its stable.
- Chamberpots were emptied into the children's beds.

Drury was arrested again for stealing a pig in Gloucester. He claimed it was his witch powers that were cursing Mompasson. So Drury was tried for witchcraft and sentenced to transportation overseas.

The haunting of Mompasson's house stopped. Drummer Drury was lucky. Twenty years earlier he would have been burnt at the stake as a witch.

Horrible Histories. 'The Slimy Stuarts' by Terry Deary

Extract 3

Haunted by a Fiddler

Position: St James' Park, King's Lynn, Norfolk.
OS Map: North West Norfolk, Sheet 132, 1:50,000.
Map ref: TF 625 198.
Access: Red Mount Chapel is on a mound on 'The Walks' in the park.

Red Mount Chapel is a superb example of the Gothic style in architecture and even boasts its own musical ghost!

Built in 1485 at the time of Henry VII, the first Tudor King, it was a stopping-off place for pilgrims on their way to Walsingham via the port of King's Lynn. Octagonal in shape, it is very small, and has three floors. The top floor is a chapel with fan tracery much like that in Cambridge's King's College.

Underneath the chapel building there is reputed to be a long tunnel (not unusual), running to Castle Rising – a distance of 18 km/12 miles (very unusual). An unfortunate, drunken fiddler once decided to explore the dark passageway with his instrument, his dog and his pint! He never reached the end of the tunnel, wherever it went, but his spirit remains and can be heard on occasions playing his tunes and singing, accompanied by the whining of his poor dog!

Places of Interest in the Neighbourhood

- The Shattered Maid's Heart (King's Lynn)
- Killed by a Pinprick (Stow Bartolph)
- Detached Church Tower (West Walton)

East Anglian Curiosities by Rick O'Brien

Extract 4

HAUNTED BRITAIN

The REAL X-Files.

ILFRACOMBE, DEVONSHIRE

The fifteenth-century Chambercombe Manor House has a haunted room which was discovered in 1869 when the owner noticed an extra window where there was no room. After a wall was broken down, a low, dark chamber was revealed with remains of tapestry still hanging on the walls and Elizabethan black carved furniture almost falling to pieces.

Behind the curtains the skeleton of a woman was found lying on the bed and since then weird sounds have been heard at night from the vicinity of this room, hidden for so long. Today the haunted room, situated between the Coat of Arms Bedroom (once used by Lady Jane Grey) and the low-beamed Victorian Bedroom, can be viewed through a hole in the wooden partition of the staircase; a strange mystery that will probably never now be solved. Perhaps it has some connection with the tunnel that ran from here to Hele Beach and was reputedly used by smugglers.

Westwell Hall Private Hotel, Ilfracombe, Devon

Unexplained Beyond Reality, October 1997

Extract 5

The Walberswick Whisperers

Years ago Walberswick was a flourishing port, but the pounding North Sea destroyed the harbour by continually blocking and shifting the outlet of the river. None the less, it is popular today with small-boat sailors, though they have to contend with a muddy foreshore and those constant strong currents.

The village itself offers idyllic views across heathland, reed-filled marshes and the sea. By day, the colours of the countryside are beautifully soft and muted, and over the years the place has attracted a great many painters, birdwatchers, walkers and golfers. By night, though, it is a very different story: for this is the domain of 'The Walberswick Whisperers'. . .

Catching the last ferry across the Blyth, as evening begins to fall and the boatman is obviously wanting to finish, can be a strange experience which mixes the picturesque with the uncanny. As the fading sun turns the shades of the landscape darker and then plunges them into shadow, the ferryman's oars gently slap in and out of the water and the sound is heightened by the stillness all around. The man himself stands in the bows of his small craft rather like the **ferryman of the Styx**, equally as upright, sombre and silent as the figure of legend.

It was, in fact, only as the boat landed on the Walberswick side that he finally answered the enquiry I had put to him earlier about the legend of the 'Whisperers'.

---

ferryman of the Styx: The Ancient Greeks believed that the River Styx separated the land of the living from the land of the dead. The ghosts of the dead would pay a ferryman to row them across the river

'Some nights hereabouts,' he said as he shipped his oars and tied the ferry up against the small jetty, 'the sky looks sort of sinister. What you'd call supernatural. [He pronounced it soopy-natural]. That's the sign for the spirits to rise up with the wind and start a mutterin'. All shapes and sizes they are, chatterin' and sighin'. We call them the "Walberswick Whisperers". You want to know any more, go and talk to some of they folk in the village.'

Having said this, the ferryman fell silent and turned on his heels and was soon gone into the gathering gloom. He was clearly not prepared to answer any more of the questions I had about the ghosts of Walberswick – in particular about the ferry's phantom passengers. 'Soopy-natural' beings were evidently not things he wanted to discuss when a good hot meal was awaiting him . . .

It was appropriately a local fisherman whom I met in the bar of the Anchor who explained the legend of the phantom ferry passengers which I could not extract from the boatman – a story which, he insisted, was familiar to many folk.

The haunting apparently came to general attention earlier this century when a visitor to Walberswick asked Old Todd, who was then the ferryman, to row him over to the Southwold side. As the man approached the small boat he passed the figures of an old man holding a small child by the hand. Seating himself in the boat, the visitor was surprised to see that Old Todd was about to pull away from the shore without the other two passengers. He suggested that the ferryman wait for them and turned round to see where the pair might be.

To his amazement, there was no sign of either – and as the boatman began to row he said quietly, almost under his breath, 'We never wait for *them*!'

The Supernatural Coast by Peter Haining

Extract 6

Diary of Thomas Raikes

26 December 1832

Captain – recounted a curious anecdote that had happened in his own family. He told it in the following words:

'It is now about fifteen months ago that Miss Manningham, **a connection** of my family, went with a party of friends to a concert at the Argyle Rooms. She appeared there to be suddenly seized with **indisposition**, and though she persisted for some time to struggle against what seemed a violent nervous affection, it became at last so oppressive, that they were obliged to send for their carriage and **conduct** her home. She was for a long time unwilling to say what was the cause of her indisposition; but, on being more earnestly questioned, she at length confessed that she had, immediately on arriving in the concert room, been terrified by a horrible vision, which unceasingly presented itself to her sight. It seemed to her as though a naked corpse was lying on the floor at her feet; the features of the face were partly covered by a cloth mantle, but enough was apparent to convince her that the body was that of Sir Joseph Yorke. Every effort was made by her friends at the time to tranquillize her mind by representing the folly of allowing such delusions to prey upon her spirits, and she thus retired to bed; but on the following day the family received the tidings of Sir Joseph Yorke having been drowned in Southampton River that very night by the oversetting of his boat, and the body was afterwards found entangled in a *boat cloak*. Here is an **authenticated** case of second sight, and of very recent date.'

The Faber Book of Diaries

a connection: someone known to the family
indisposition: illness   **conduct**: lead
authenticated: reliable/genuine

Activities

1   Re-read 'The Terror of Tedworth' (pages 20–21).
    Write a newspaper article about the events that
    happened after William Drury escaped. Use the
    headline:

    DRUM GHOST EXPOSED!

2   Re-read 'Haunted by a Fiddler' (page 22). At the
    end of this guide to Red Mount Chapel three other
    places of interest are listed. Write your own guide
    to one of these places. You will have to make up
    the information, but be imaginative and use the Red
    Mount Chapel guide to help you with the structure
    and presentation of your writing.

3   Imagine that you have spent the night at either
    Westwell Hall Private Hotel at Ilfracombe or the
    Anchor at Walberswick. Write an account of your
    stay, describing a strange and mysterious experience
    that happened during the night. Use the information
    from either text to help you to write your account.
    At the end of your piece of writing you may wish to
    give a logical explanation of the events.

4   Read 'The Walberswick Whisperers' again (pages
    24–25). Although the writer visited Walberswick to
    investigate the mysterious Whisperers, in the end he
    wrote very little about them. Imagine that you have
    been asked to contribute to a Supernatural Fact File.
    Write your own entry for the Whisperers.

5   Look back at the cartoon strip 'Chopped Charlie's
    Last Chance' (pages 19–20). Now produce your own
    cartoon strip to describe the events recorded by

Thomas Raikes in his diary, and make it funny by using modern language for the speech bubbles.

6 Using the information from all the texts in this section, produce a Frights' Frieze. Draw and label each ghost or apparition described in the texts. Work in groups, using large pieces of paper to produce a display for your classroom.

Section 3
Ourselves and Other Animals

This section is about the different relationships that exist between human beings and animals. By reading the extracts you will discover how animals are treated: as pets, as captives, as objects of study, and occasionally as free creatures.

Read the introductions and extracts which follow before working through the activities on pages 45–47.

Extract 1: Rabbits Indoors (page 31) **and Exercise** (page 33)

These two short extracts are taken from a book called *How to Look After Your Rabbit*. It is an information book designed to appeal to young children.

Extract 2: Pets (page 35)

Michael Rosen is well known for the amusing poems he writes for children. However, this piece of writing is taken from his book, *An A–Z Guide to Fatherhood Goodies and Daddies*, which is an information book about looking after babies and young children.

Extract 3: It Will Be Gone by October (page 36)

This advertisement appeared in the *BBC Wildlife Magazine*. What do you think it is advertising?

Extract 4: Fly Away Home (page 37)

This is an article taken from the magazine, *Wildlife Times*, which is produced by the Born Free Foundation. The Born Free Foundation is a charity set up to save individual wild and captive animals. In this article Tricia Holford describes how two captive lions were returned to the wild.

Extract 5: The Aye-Aye and I (page 42)

Gerald Durrell was an explorer, a collector of wild animals, and the owner of the Jersey Zoo and Wildlife Preservation Trust. In order to fund his collecting expeditions, and later his zoo, Durrell began writing books based on his experiences with animals. This extract is taken from an account of a major collecting expedition in Madagascar.

Extract 6: Chimpanzee (page 43)

This is an entry taken from *The British World Book Encyclopaedia* about the chimpanzee.

Extract 7: Diary of Anne Chalmers – 22 May 1830 (page 44)

Little is known about this Victorian lady who kept a diary for just one year. This diary entry records a trip she made to London Zoo. In 1830 the Zoo was open only to Fellows of the Society and their guests, so Anne Chalmers must have known some important people to have been able to make this visit.

Extract 1

Rabbits Indoors

If your pet lives indoors she will need her own cosy sleeping box lined with hay, where she can rest at any time.

I really like living indoors.

carrot juice

toast

comfy chair

A rabbit makes a very good indoor pet and can be trained to use a litter tray. You can use ordinary cat litter.

Do you mind! This is a private poo!

If your rabbit is used to living in the house be careful that she doesn't escape when you open an outside door. She may never come back!

Watch out that your rabbit does not nibble through wires; she could get an electric shock. Pet shops sell a spray which you can use to coat any visible wires. It tastes unpleasant and will stop unwanted nibbling.

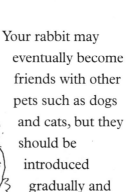

Your rabbit may eventually become friends with other pets such as dogs and cats, but they should be introduced gradually and you may have to be patient.

Exercise

A fit bunny is a healthy bunny.

Like all animals, rabbits need exercise to stay fit and healthy, and an outdoor run is an excellent place for your pet to play and nibble grass in safety.

This type of run is called an ark and can be made or bought. Make sure you put it in the shade and always attach a water bottle to the outside. Move the ark every day so that the rabbit has fresh grass to nibble and never put it on grass that has been treated with weedkiller.

An ark should have a shelter at one end and wire netting on the bottom to stop your pet burrowing out and other animals, such as foxes, from digging in.

Make sure your rabbit is not bothered by other pets . . .

and don't leave her in the run at night or in bad weather.

Even if she has been nibbling grass all day, you should still give your pet the usual amount of food at her regular feeding time.

Extract 2

Pets

Young children love pets. Pets don't always love children. Great big dogs seem to think they're very important, and protect them from strangers. One Great Dane I knew (!) would never let a stranger stand between the mother and the baby in its pram. It wasn't aggressive, it just nudged in and made sure you couldn't get near. Just as well it wasn't aggressive – it was about as big as a donkey.

Cats don't seem to be useful. Young children like poking cats, and cats seem to think that a poke is worth at least a spit and at worst a scratch. Small children and cats clearly weren't designed to be good friends.

Gerbils are a winner if you feel you can look after them as well as a baby, but all young children are animal liberationists in so far as they are very keen on opening cage doors.

Beware of dog do. It is lethal, terrible stuff. Young teething children will quite happily chew a shoe or suck their fingers after they've fallen over in the park. Dog do can carry eggs of a parasite that can make children blind. It's a terrifying thought. You have to be vigilant about it.

Look out for jealous pets. They get all down-at-the-mouth and whiny. If you're holding the baby, a dog will sometimes come up and put its nose on your lap to say, 'me, too'. Pets must be kept out of the room where the baby is sleeping. Cats will sleep on babies and possibly suffocate them, dogs might bite, and gerbils . . .well, who knows? Jealous gerbils . . .what an idea.

An A–Z Guide to Fatherhood Goodies and Daddies
by Michael Rosen

Extract 3

It Will Be Gone by October

The September issue of *BBC Wildlife Magazine* is an endangered species special.

So you'll have to act fast if you want to find out more about animals under threat such as black rhinos, Siamese crocodiles or Yangtze River dolphins. Because before you know it, the September issue will have gone from the shelves forever. And you wouldn't want to miss the features on the 13 most endangered species, on the pygmy hogs and Przewalski's wild horses, thought to be extinct in the wild and now rediscovered in Mongolia.

If you care about endangered species, act now. Hurry down to your local newsagent before it's too late.

BBC Wildlife Magazine

Extract 4

FLY AWAY HOME

ON 1ST APRIL, 1995, TWO LIONS ARRIVED AT MALCOLM
DUDDING'S SANCTUARY IN KENT. RESCUED BY THE BFF
FROM A ROOFTOP BAR IN TENERIFE, LITTLE DID WE
KNOW THAT TWO YEARS LATER THEY WOULD BEGIN A
NEW LIFE IN AN AFRICAN GAME RESERVE. TRICIA
HOLFORD, MANAGER OF THE BIG CAT PROJECT,
CO-ORDINATED THE MOVE AND REPORTS BACK ON
EVENTS IN THE AFRICAN BUSH.

The two lions lay on their backs in the shade of an acacia tree, their massive paws limp and relaxed. We had been watching them for 20 minutes when the male slowly stood up, stretched, and padded over to a clearing. He began to roar. It was a deep, heart-stopping roar which echoed along the ancient African valley. It was an announcement that he, Raffi, had arrived and it was his territory now. Slowly he returned to his mate and lay peacefully beside her. It was quiet once more.

FIRST ENCOUNTER

It was a dramatic contrast to my first encounter with them on a Tenerife rooftop in 1994. That image of two thin, grubby lions pacing back and forth in their tiny cage is forever etched in my memory. The corrugated iron roof turned the cage into an oven. Without a water bowl in sight, the only features in the tiny cage were an old rubbish bin and narrow sleeping shelf with nails sticking out. For five years Raffi and Anthea had mentally survived in these conditions – how? I never believed that I would one day see them in their ancestral home.

CHANCE MEETING

It was the stuff of fairy tales and all down to a chance meeting between Richard Hedges from Britannia Airways and Adrian Gardiner, owner of Shamwari Game Reserve. Britannia Airways played a key role in the Tenerife rescue, flying the lions from Spain to England. Having recently added South Africa to their list of destinations, Richard was checking on a new tourist venue he had heard about. The Shamwari Game Reserve was, until six years ago, 30,000 acres of arid farmland. Now, thanks to Adrian Gardiner's vision, it had become lush natural habitat. A new home for many hundreds of animals that were once indigenous to the area.

Richard told Adrian how Britannia had helped the BFF rescue Raffi and Anthea. Adrian was so moved that he immediately offered the lions a new 'home for life' at Shamwari. This would include the construction of a special enclosure in the African bush. As if that wasn't enough, Britannia offered to cover all the flight expenses and travel arrangements. Britannia flew a BFF team to

Shamwari to check out the facilities. Discussions about transport logistics, veterinary cover, diet plans and security were made with Shamwari vet Dr John Joubert. The decision was then made to go ahead with the move.

The next step was to obtain formal approval from the Spanish government. This was swiftly granted and everyone swung into action. In less than a month it was the day of departure.

26th March 5p.m.

A small crowd of journalists, well-wishers and staff gathered outside Raffi and Anthea's indoor quarters. John Kenward, the veterinary surgeon, disappeared inside to administer the anaesthetic dart. First Raffi, then Anthea were anaesthetized and put into their travelling crates. It was an emotional time for the sanctuary staff who had cared so well for the lions over the past two years – a few tears were shed. The crates were carefully loaded on to a Britannia Airways lorry, the vet reversed their anaesthetic and two drowsy lions were soon en route to Gatwick Airport.

NEXT STOP AFRICA

28th March 7a.m.

Virginia McKenna and I stood outside Raffi and Anthea's new enclosure waiting for their lorry to arrive. Everything was ready. The lions were travelling overland from Mombasa, accompanied by John the vet, Tony Wiles, our manager at the sanctuary, and John O'Brien, Shamwari's head ranger. Our mobile phone rang. The lorry and its precious cargo had reached Shamwari and would be with us in 10 minutes. The anticipation and excitement in the air was almost tangible.

Virginia McKenna takes up the story:
'The lorry drove into the enclosure. The engine was switched off. Silence. I imagined the sense of relief the lions might experience after 36 hours of relentless noise. The crates were gently lowered to the ground, the sliding doors raised and Raffi bounded out. Some people cheered, some wept. He looked wonderful. Sniffing the warm air he gazed around and then, as if to reassure her, returned towards Anthea who was still in her crate. She too emerged vigorously but began a fast pacing movement at the fence line. Meanwhile Raffi had wandered off to the far end of the enclosure and we decided to leave them for a while to settle in. Shamwari's vet stayed behind to keep an eye on them.'

A NEW LIFE BEGINS

During our days at Shamwari, the BFF team monitored Raffi and Anthea's reaction to their new home. Their old affectionate habits returned and the playful pair began to explore the three acres of African bush. Anthea's strange rocking-horse gait, the result of her Tenerife confinement, seemed almost unnoticeable. Even though the Shamwari enclosure is 1,667 times larger than their rooftop prison, it will be enlarged if it doesn't satisfy their inquisitive natures.

A FOND FAREWELL

Our last day arrived and it was time for 'goodbyes'. In the cool mist of the African sunrise, we saw two feline noses peeping from the undergrowth. Raffi and Anthea made no attempt to come over as they had done before. Their new life had begun. Virginia's words summed up our feelings exactly: 'It has been a long journey from Tenerife to Shamwari. I was unashamedly emotional when Anthea and Raffi stepped, at last, on to the African soil and I knew they had finally "come home". Without question this has been, for me, the happiest outcome of all our endeavours over the years. We could never have dreamed that, one day, the lions' tiny cement and barred cell would be transformed into three acres of African bush. But sometimes, with the help of friends, dreams do come true.'

Wildlife Times

Extract 5

THE AYE-AYE AND I

In the gloom it came along the branches towards me, its round, hypnotic eyes blazing, its spoon-like ears turning to and fro independently like radar dishes, its white whiskers twitching and moving like sensors; its black hands, with their thin, attenuated fingers, the third seeming prodigiously elongated, tapping delicately on the branches as it moved along, like those of a pianist playing a complicated piece by Chopin. It looked like a Walt Disney witch's black cat with a touch of E.T. thrown in for good measure. If ever a flying saucer came from Mars, you felt that this is what would emerge from it. It was Lewis Carroll's Jabberwocky come to life, wiffling through its tulgey wood.

It lowered itself on to my shoulder, gazed into my face with its huge, hypnotic eyes and ran slender fingers through my beard and hair as gently as any barber. In its underslung jaw, I could see giant chisel-like teeth, teeth which grow constantly, and I sat quite still. It uttered a small, snorting noise like 'humph' and descended to my lap. Here, it inspected my walking-stick. Its black fingers played along its length as if the stick were a flute. Then it leant forward and, with alarming accuracy, almost bisected my stick with two bites from its enormous teeth. To its obvious chagrin, it found no beetle larvae there and so it returned to my shoulder. Again, it combed my beard and hair, gentle as a baby breeze.

Then, to my alarm, it discovered my ear. 'Here,' it seemed to say to itself, 'must lurk a beetle larva of royal proportions and of the utmost succulence.' It fondled my ear as a gourmet fondles a menu and then, with great care, it inserted its thin finger. I resigned myself to deafness – move over, Beethoven, I said to myself, here I come. To my astonishment, I could hardly feel the finger as it searched my ear like a radar probe for hidden delicacies. Finding my ear bereft of tasty and fragrant grubs, it uttered another faint 'humph' of annoyance and climbed up into the branches again.

The Best of Gerald Durrell

Extract 6

Chimpanzee

Chimpanzee is an African Ape. Chimpanzees are one of the four kinds of apes, along with gibbons, gorillas, and orang-utans. The chimpanzee ranks as one of the most intelligent animals and resembles human beings more closely than any other animal does.

Chimpanzees have many characteristics that make them interesting and valuable to human beings. Its playfulness and curiosity make it a popular animal at zoos. Young chimpanzees can be tamed and trained easily, and they make excellent circus performers. Scientists use them in medical and psychological research because the animals have many similarities to humans.

The British World Book Encyclopaedia

Extract 7

Diary of Anne Chalmers

22 May 1830

We walked to the Zoological Garden in Regent's Park. It is a most delightful spectacle, the animals have so much more liberty than in common menageries. The enclosures are large, and all except the wild animals are kept in the open air during the daytime. The tiger seemed to feel annoyed at being looked on in what it esteemed a state of degradation, and walked up and down its narrow prison as if it would fain increase its boundaries, and the lion lay asleep – perhaps dreaming of its own native forests, or of a delicious banquet which it tasted only *once*, but remembers with continued zest, consisting of a young negro which had been brought to it by its mother. Many more animals and birds were there than I can enumerate, but I shall mention the monkeys, whose tricks were very diverting. I brought them some nuts and biscuits, and whenever they saw them there was a commotion in their cages, and paws were stretched out in all directions for them. While I was bending to give a weak one a nut, which a superior was taking from it, my bonnet was seized from a cage above and the front nearly torn from it. The keeper let them out from their confinement into large arbours in the open air, where were hung swings and ropes, and certainly the gymnastics of the Greenwich boys were far exceeded by these agile creatures. They flung themselves from rope to rope and to the side of the cage with immense celerity. Next in agility to the monkeys were the bears, though in a more clumsy style. They begged for buns, and clambered up a long pole to amuse the bystanders, who rewarded them with cakes. Mamma was quite pleased with the beaver for showing itself both on land and water, she said it was very obliging and exceedingly gentlemanly of it.

Activities

1 **a** Use the information from 'Rabbits Indoors' and 'Exercise' (pages 31–34) to write a short story about a pet rabbit. You may use the following sentences to start your story:

> *There was once a young rabbit named Mavis who spent all her nights in a hutch, and all her days in an outdoor run. Mavis was a happy bunny until, one day, a new cat moved into the neighbourhood.*
> *'Hello, bunny!' purred the cat, licking his lips.*

b Write your own information sheet about feeding pet rabbits. Remember, you are writing for young children so keep your writing clear and simple, and include some funny drawings. Here are a few facts which you could include in your writing:
- Rabbits are herbivores
- Dry food pellets are nutritious
- Feed fresh greens daily
- Some rabbits like fruit
- Hay is important
- Rabbits need fresh water.

2 Re-read the extract, 'Pets' (page 35). It is written in a light, amusing style, but Michael Rosen is also making some important points about the dangers pets can pose for very young children. In your own words, list the problems. For example: Dogs can be over-protective.

3 The advertisement for the *BBC Wildlife Magazine*, 'It Will Be Gone by October' (page 36), cleverly uses a combination of picture, headline and text to persuade readers to buy the magazine. In order to help you to understand how the advertisement works, copy and complete the following.

This picture shows ....

....

It is effective because ....

....

The headline seems to be referring to ....

.... ,

but is actually about ....

....

The text (writing) links the rhino with the magazine by using words such as ....

....

4 **a** Re-read the article 'Fly Away Home' (pages 37–41). Make a list of all the people, or organizations, who were involved with the release of the lions into the Shamwari Game Reserve. Next to each name write notes about what each person or organization did. For example:

Britannia Airways	Flew lions from Spain to England Flew lions from Gatwick to . . .

b Work in groups of four. One of you should take the role of a reporter sent by a television company to find out as much as possible about the release of the lions. The rest of the group should take the roles of three of the people from your list. Act out the interview.

c As a whole class, perhaps with your teacher in the role of the programme controller, the reporters should talk briefly about what they have found out. The rest of the class may ask the reporters questions.

5 a Re-read the extract from 'The Aye-Aye and I' (pages 42–43). List all the facts that it gives you about the Aye-Aye. For example:

The Aye-Aye can climb trees.

b Now look again at the extract, 'Chimpanzee' (page 43). Using all the facts you have gathered in question 5a, write your own entry for the Aye-Aye for *The British World Book Encyclopaedia*.

6 Our views about keeping wild animals in captivity have changed considerably since Anne Chalmers wrote her diary in 1830.

a Make a list of the main 'delightful spectacle[s]' that Anne Chalmers writes about.

b Make notes about how you feel about each 'spectacle'.

c Imagine you are able to send a piece of writing back through time to 1830. Use your notes to write a letter to the Zoological Garden (London Zoo) in which you protest about the way the animals are treated, and suggest ways in which their condition may be improved.

Section 4
Travel

Imagine what it must be like to travel to the moon, or to take part in a high-speed car rally. Yet in 1830 even a ride in a steam engine was an exciting event for Anne Chalmers. In this section you can read Anne's diary entry in which she writes about the thrill of travelling at 34 miles per hour! Read also three accounts written by people who were on board the *Titanic* the day she sank; and decide whether the Inter-Rail pamphlet would persuade you to take the train.

Read the introductions and extracts which follow before working through the activities on pages 63–66.

Extract 1: The Ride of Your Life (page 51)

This is an information pamphlet about rail travel in Europe.

Extract 2: Advantage Subaru (page 54)

In this magazine article, written for the September 1997 edition of *Rally Sport*, Martin Holmes describes the opening stages of the World Championship race held in New Zealand.

Extract 3: Stories from the *Titanic* (page 55)

The *Titanic* was a luxury liner which set sail in 1912, and sank on her very first voyage. 1,513 people drowned because there were not enough lifeboats. This extract contains three eye-witness accounts of what happened.

Extract 4: The First Men on the Moon, 21 July 1969
(page 60)

Neil Armstrong and Edwin Aldrin were the first men to land on the moon. In this extract, Armstrong and Aldrin describe some memorable moments of their fantastic adventure.

Extract 5: Diary of Anne Chalmers – 25 June 1830
(page 62)

In this entry of 25 June 1830 Anne Chalmers writes about her experience of travelling in a 'waggon' pulled by one of the first steam locomotives.

Extract 1

the ride of your life

freedom - Get out and use it

You can get into Europe in a big way with an Inter-Rail Pass. Europe's opened up, barriers are down, countries and cultures are being rediscovered. There's never been a better or more exciting time to travel and experience those changes first hand – a chance to challenge your preconceptions about places and people, and have a fantastic time into the bargain.

All there for the taking

You can enjoy unlimited rail travel in 27 countries in Europe and one in Africa – Morocco. And, as you'll discover, there's nothing quite like a train journey for getting to know the locals, what's on, what's going on and where else to go.

Troll around in the B zone

Take a fortnight out and explore Scandinavia. A discounted ferry to Gothenburg gets you started on a spectacular scenic tour taking in the excitement of Helsinki, Stockholm and Oslo. And while you're there don't miss out on a once-in-a-lifetime train ride across the Arctic Circle.

Streetwise and Wherefores

Make sure you're well insured against the cost of accidents and loss of property. And that includes your Inter-Rail Pass, as it can't be replaced. We have a policy specially designed and recommended for Inter-Railers – reassuring for you and your family should anything untoward happen.

Brass in pocket

Don't get caught out of pocket, make sure you're carrying currency for each country you're likely to visit on your journey.

Ensure you order currency for East European countries 24 hrs in advance. And take a variety of payment methods, credit cards, travellers' cheques as well as cash. Thomas Cook also offer the MoneyGram service which means that in an emergency relatives or friends back home can send you money overseas in less than 10 minutes.

Speed Freaks join here

Your Inter-Rail Pass gets you everywhere and anywhere in Europe. But for a supplement you can enjoy high-speed services like the TGV. You might need to make a reservation for some Continental trains, so check things out in the Thomas Cook European Rail timetable for details.

Rail Europe
International Rail Centre, Victoria Station,
London SW1V 1JY

Tel: 0990 848848

Inter-Rail pamphlet

Extract 2

Advantage Subaru

After the mid-season break, Mitsubishi, Subaru and Ford continued the battle for the World Championship title in New Zealand. Martin Holmes didn't mind wasting two days of his life in a plane to follow the action!

The rally started with a major attack by Colin McRae, who led for the first eight stages, and Tommi Mäkinen who pushed him hard. On stage four Mäkinen crashed heavily when his car slid into the apex of a fast corner and the sumpguard dug into the mud, then Colin's engine stopped without warning on stage nine. The rally then became wide open, and Carlos was in the lead for two stages.

On stage 11, at 47 km the longest of the event, he made a wrong tyre choice, as did most of the Michelin users. He slithered around in the later stretches of the stage, spun momentarily, and dropped a quarter-minute behind Eriksson. A local journalist asked the Swede if the race for victory was now ended. 'No. The battle is only just beginning!'

Rally Sport

Extract 3

Stories from the *Titanic*

●

The Titanic: *A Fireman's Story,*
15 April 1912

The 'unsinkable' Titanic had only 1,178 lifeboat spaces for the 2,224 people aboard. A total of 1,513 lives were lost – a high proportion of them steerage passengers.

I was in my bunk when I felt a bump. One man said, 'Hello. She has been struck.' I went on deck and saw a great pile of ice on the well deck before the forecastle, but we all thought the ship would last some time, and we went back to our bunks. Then one of the firemen came running down and yelled, 'All muster for the lifeboats.' I ran on deck, and the Captain said, 'All firemen keep down on the well deck. If a man comes up I'll shoot him.'

Then I saw the first lifeboat lowered. Thirteen people were on board, eleven men and two women. Three were millionaires, and one was Ismay [J. Bruce Ismay, Managing Director of the White Star Line; a survivor].

Then I ran up on to the hurricane deck and helped to throw one of the collapsible boats on to the lower deck. I saw an Italian woman holding two babies. I took one of them, and made the woman jump overboard with the baby, while I did the same with the other. When I came to the surface the baby in my arms was dead. I saw the woman strike out in good style, but a boiler burst on the *Titanic* and started a big wave. When the woman saw that wave, she gave up. Then, as the child was dead, I let it sink too.

---

forecastle: a short raised deck at the bow (front) of the ship

I swam around for about half an hour, and was swimming on my back when the *Titanic* went down. I tried to get aboard a boat, but some chap hit me over the head with an oar. There were too many in her. I got around to the other side of the boat and climbed in.

Harry Senior

●

The Titanic: *The Wireless Operator's Story, 15 April 1912*

From **aft** came the tunes of the band. It was a ragtime tune. I don't know what. Then there was 'Autumn'. . . . I went to the place I had seen the collapsible boat on the boat deck, and to my surprise I saw the boat, and the men still trying to push it off. I guess there wasn't a sailor in the crowd. They couldn't do it. I went up to them and was just lending a hand when a large wave came awash of the deck. The big wave carried the boat off. I had hold of an oarlock and I went with it. The next I knew I was in the boat. But that was not all. I was in the boat, and the boat was upside-down, and I was under it. And I remember realizing I was wet through and that whatever happened I must not breathe, for I was under water. I knew I had to fight for it, and I did. How I got out from under the boat I do not know but I felt a breath of air at last. There were men all around me – hundreds of them. The sea was dotted with them, all depending on their lifebelts. I felt I simply had to get away from the ship. She was a beautiful sight then. Smoke and sparks were rushing out of her funnel. There must have been an explosion, but we heard none. We only saw the big stream of sparks. The ship was turning gradually on her

aft: towards the stern of the ship

nose – just like a duck that goes for a dive. I had only one thing on my mind – to get away from the suction. The band was still playing. I guess all of them went down. They were playing 'Autumn' then. I swam with all my might. I suppose I was 150 feet away when the *Titanic*, on her nose, with her after-quarter sticking straight up in the air, began to settle – slowly.

When at last the waves washed over her rudder there wasn't the least bit of suction I could feel. She must have kept going just so slowly as she had been . . . I felt after a little while like sinking. I was very cold. I saw a boat of some kind near me, and put all my strength into an effort to swim to it. It was hard work. I was all done when a hand reached out from the boat and pulled me aboard. It was our same collapsible. The same crowd was on it. There was just room for me to roll on the edge. I lay there not caring what happened. Somebody sat on my legs. They were wedged in between slats and were being wrenched. I had not the heart left to ask the man to move. It was a terrible sight all around – men swimming and sinking.

I lay where I was, letting the man wrench my feet out of shape. Others came near. Nobody gave them a hand. The bottom-up boat already had more men than it would hold, and it was sinking. At first the larger waves splashed over my clothing. Then they began to splash over my head, and I had to breathe when I could. As we floated around on our capsized boat and I kept straining my eyes for a ship's lights, somebody said, 'Don't the rest of you think we ought to pray?' The man who made the suggestion asked what the religion of the others was. Each man called out his religion. One was a Catholic, one a Methodist, one a Presbyterian. It was decided the most appropriate prayer for all was the Lord's Prayer. We spoke it over in chorus with the man who first suggested that we pray as the leader. Some splendid people saved us. They had a right-side-up boat and it was full to capacity. Yet they came to us and loaded us all into it. I saw some lights off in the distance and knew a steamship was coming to our aid.

Harold Bride

●

The Titanic: *From a Lifeboat, 15 April 1912*

We did not begin to understand the situation till we were perhaps a mile or more away from the *Titanic*. Then we could see the rows of lights along the decks begin to slant gradually upward from the bow. Very slowly the lines of light began to point downward at a greater and greater angle. The sinking was so slow that you could not perceive the lights of the deck changing their position. The slant seemed to be greater about every quarter of an hour. That was the only difference.

In a couple of hours, though, she began to go down more rapidly. Then the fearful sight began. The people in the ship were just beginning to realize how great their danger was. When the forward part of the ship dropped suddenly at a faster rate, so that the upward slope became marked, there was a sudden rush of passengers on all the decks towards the stern. It was like a wave. We could see the great black mass of people in the **steerage** sweeping to the rear part of the boat and breaking through into the upper decks. At the distance of about a mile we could distinguish everything through the night, which was perfectly clear. We could make out the increasing excitement on board the boat as the people, rushing to

---

steerage: the cheapest part of the ship for passengers to travel in

and fro, caused the deck lights to disappear and reappear as they passed in front of them.

This panic went on, it seemed, for an hour. Then suddenly the ship seemed to shoot up out of the water and stand there **perpendicularly**. It seemed to us that it stood upright in the water for four full minutes.

Then it began to slide gently downwards. Its speed increased as it went down head first, so that the stern shot down with a rush.

The lights continued to burn till it sank. We could see the people packed densely in the stern till it was gone . . .

As the ship sank we could hear the screaming a mile away. Gradually it became fainter and fainter and died away. Some of the lifeboats that had room for more might have gone to their rescue, but it would have meant that those who were in the water would have swarmed aboard and sunk her.

Mrs D. H. Bishop

The Faber Book of Reportage

---

perpendicularly: at right angles to the horizon/upright

Extract 4

The First Men on the Moon, 21 July 1969

Apollo II, carrying Neil Armstrong, Lieutenant-Colonel Michael Collins, and Colonel Edwin Aldrin, was launched on 16 July. At 03.56 BST on 21 July Armstrong stepped off the ladder of lunar landing vehicle Eagle on to the Moon.

Neil Armstrong: The most dramatic recollections I had were the sights themselves. Of all the spectacular views we had, the most impressive to me was on the way to the Moon, when we flew through its shadow. We were still thousands of miles away, but close enough, so that the Moon almost filled our circular window. It was eclipsing the Sun, from our position, and the corona of the Sun was visible around the limb of the Moon as a gigantic lens-shaped or saucer-shaped light, stretching out to several lunar diameters. It was magnificent, but the Moon was even more so. We were in its shadow, so there was no part of it illuminated by the Sun. It was illuminated only by earthshine. It made the Moon appear blue-grey, and the entire scene looked decidedly three-dimensional.

I was really aware, visually aware, that the Moon was in fact a sphere not a disc. It seemed almost as if it were showing us its roundness, its similarity in shape to our Earth, in a sort of welcome. I was sure that it would be a hospitable host. It had been awaiting its first visitors for a long time . . .

[*After touchdown*] The sky is black, you know.

It's a very dark sky. But it still seemed more like daylight than darkness as we looked out the window. It's a peculiar thing, but the surface looked very warm and inviting. It was the sort of situation in which you felt like going out there in nothing but a swimming suit to get a little sun. From the cockpit, the surface seemed to be tan. It's hard to account for that, because later when I held this material in my hand, it wasn't tan at all. It was black, grey and so on. It's some kind of lighting effect, but out the window the surface looks much more like light desert sand than black sand . . .

Edwin E. Aldrin [*on the moon*]: The blue colour of my boots has completely disappeared now into this – still don't know exactly what colour to describe this other than greyish-cocoa colour. It appears to be covering most of the lighter part of my boot . . . very fine particles . . .

Odour is very subjective, but to me there was a distinct smell to the lunar material – pungent, like gunpowder or spent cap-pistol caps. We carted a fair amount of lunar dust back inside the vehicle with us, either on our suits and boots or on the conveyor system we used to get boxes and equipment back inside. We did notice the odour right away.

The Faber Book of Reportage

Extract 5

Diary of Anne Chalmers

25 June 1830

Breakfasted at eleven o'clock, and then set off in a carriage with Mr Hoffender, Papa, and Mary Rose, although it was pouring with rain, to have a drive in a steam engine. Mr Charles and Pat rode in the **phaeton**. Upon arriving at the destined spot we climbed a steep bank to await its arrival, but after standing in the rain for some time we were told it had passed an hour before, so we returned the way we came; but before we had gone far we passed the railroad and saw the steam engine **in propria persona**. There had been some mistake about it which I did not take the trouble to **comprehend**, but we got into the waggon and rode five miles in it in ten minutes, sometimes faster and sometimes slower, and once at the rate of thirty-four miles an hour. The motion is **imperceptible**, and the feeling of moving so quickly most exhilarating; we wrote each a sentence while we were at full speed, and would have done so with perfect ease had not the rain, which was very heavy, blotted the writing. Afterwards we went to the entrance of the tunnel and met there Mr De Cappleton and Mr Scoresby. We here entered a waggon, and being pushed off, the motion accelerated, and we passed through the tunnel one mile and a quarter in four minutes.

The Faber Book of Diaries

---

phaeton: a light, four-wheeled, open carriage
in propria persona: the real thing
comprehend: understand
imperceptible: not noticeable / very slight

Activities

1 Look again at 'The Ride of Your Life' (pages 51–53) and then copy and complete the following prompt sheet.

The pamphlet 'The Ride of Your Life' is produced by

....

The following words and phrases have been chosen because they are eye-catching:

....

....

These words and phrases make the idea of rail

travel seem ....

The sub-headings are ....

The pamphlet persuades readers to

....

The pamphlet is designed to appeal to

....

Now re-write the pamphlet so that it would appeal to a nervous traveller.

- Give the pamphlet a title.
- Choose your sub-headings.
- Choose your words carefully to emphasize the safety, comfort and reliability of rail travel.

2 Try reading the extract 'Advantage Subaru' (page 54) aloud as if you are:

- an excited race commentator
- a disapproving spectator.

Before each reading, decide which words you will need to emphasize.

3   a   Re-read Harry Senior's account of the sinking of the *Titanic* (pages 55–56).

- Where was Harry Senior when the ship struck the iceberg?
- Who was in the first lifeboat?
- Why do you think the Italian woman with the two babies was *not* in a lifeboat?
- Why was Harry hit over the head with an oar?

  b   Look again at Harold Bride's account (pages 56–58).

- What happened to the band who were playing on board the *Titanic?*
- How did Harold Bride reach the collapsible boat?
- How was Harold Bride finally rescued?

Imagine you were the person in the 'collapsible' who pulled Harold to safety. Write your own account of what happened.

  c   Re-read Mrs Bishop's account from one of the lifeboats (pages 58–59).

- What did Mrs Bishop learn from the movement of the lights on the decks of the *Titanic*?

- Describe the movements of the *Titanic* as it began to sink.

4 a Look back at 'The First Men on the Moon' (pages 60–61). Working in pairs, make a list of questions you would like to be able to ask Neil Armstrong and Edwin Aldrin. Set your questions out in a table like the one below.

Questions	Answers
What is a corona?	
How did you feel when __?	

b When you have finished writing your questions, exchange your work with another pair and try to fill in the answers. You may need to use other reference books, such as an encyclopaedia, to help you find the answers.

5 a In her diary entry (page 62), Anne Chalmers describes the sequence of events that happened that day, but she says very little about her feelings. Copy and complete the following table. Use the text to complete the first column, and your imagination to complete the second.

Sequence of events	Anne's thoughts and feelings
Breakfast at eleven o'clock	*I was feeling a little nervous about the day ahead. Left my toast, but managed a sip of tea.*

b   Use the notes from your table to write an alternative diary entry about what happened that day. Write as if you are Anne Chalmers, and this time include your fears, worries, excitement etc.

6 a   Working in pairs, make a set of Trivial Pursuit-type question cards based on the information in all the texts to be found in this section. Write each question on a separate card. Write the answer upside-down on the bottom of the card.

Example

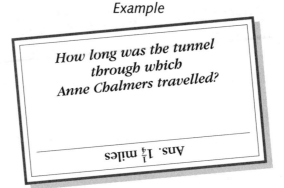

How long was the tunnel through which Anne Chalmers travelled?

Ans. 1¼ miles

b   Join up with another pair. Lay the cards face down. Take turns to pick a card and ask the question. Score one point for each correct answer.

Section 5
Early Years, Early Problems

Most of us will have had an experience in our childhood which stands out in our memory for whatever reason. It may be an exciting event, an embarrassing moment or a terrible occasion which we would much rather forget. In this section the three pieces of non-fiction are all extracts from autobiographies in which the authors tell us about a memorable event from their childhoods.

Read the introductions and extracts which follow before working through the activities on pages 79–80.

Extract 1: from *Fear of the Collar* by Patrick Touher (page 69)

When Patrick Touher was eight years old he was sent to a boarding school known as 'Artane Industrial School'. In his book, *Fear of the Collar*, Touher describes his experiences at this school. The school was famous in Ireland because every boy was taught a skilled trade, but also because it was the 'most feared school in the country'. In the extract on page 69 he describes the day he was sent away to the school.

Extract 2: from *Forever England* by Beryl Bainbridge (page 72)

Beryl Bainbridge usually writes novels, but in *Forever England* she has chosen to write about real people in real places. In the extract on page 72 she writes about the unpleasant memories of her fourteenth birthday.

Extract 3: from ***And None Of It Was Nonsense*** by
Betty Rosen (page 75)

Betty Rosen is a teacher who loves her job. In her book,
And None Of It Was Nonsense she describes how she
taught story-telling in a school that 'had a bad reputation'.
The book has been written for other teachers to read and
enjoy, but I am sure that you too will enjoy this extract in
which she recalls her favourite childhood story-book and
an incident from her own school days.

Extract 1

Extract from
Fear of the Collar

Margaret proceeded to dress me in the new clothes –
new underwear, a new suit, new shoes and new socks.
I noticed tears in her eyes and then she whispered to
me that I was being sent away, for how long she could
not say, or to where she was not sure. She thought it
was to a hospital or a very big school. Margaret was
just like a loving big sister to me.

I was all dressed up now, looking very smart and
feeling very odd. I knew something was happening. I
began to feel that I was about to travel, destination
unknown. I ran from the bedroom to the kitchen
where Roseanna was making the tea. 'Please tell me
where I'm going,' I pleaded. 'Please give me a hint
even. Is it good or bad?' Roseanna said, 'Be quiet now!
You'll find out soon enough. Sit down there and eat
your porridge. You'll need it where you're going.' I
said, 'Where's that, Mam?'

Margaret looked at her mother as she went to sit
down. I noticed the nod and wink. Roseanna then
said, 'You'll be going to the hospital as soon as
the car arrives.' 'Hospital!' I cried. 'What's a hospital,
Margaret? Is it like something you were telling me
about? Like a big school, sort of, with priests and
nuns?' 'Well, not really,' Margaret said, 'but it is as big,
yes.'

'The hospital has doctors and nurses,' Roseanna
butted in, and then said, 'You'll be going there to get
your tonsils looked at, and maybe to get them out.' I
felt just as confused as before. I ate my porridge that

morning with a kind of fear in me, a fear of the unknown, a feeling I had never experienced before. But I still ate up two bowls of porridge and lots of homemade buttermilk bread.

Though I was very young, I could tell when something was wrong in the house. I felt now everyone was watching me and saying very little. A nod or a wink, oh, sure, I could see it in their eyes, I tell you. Margaret was very upset, as was Roseanna, and Mr Doyle was very quiet, sitting in his armchair, puffing away at his pipe. Mr Doyle seemed quite old to me. He was a tall straight man. His son John was just as tall and straight and looked like his father.

The clock over the fireplace struck nine. I heard Roseanna saying to Margaret, as they washed up after the breakfast, 'It should be here now.' Then I heard a car pull up outside the cottage door. I noticed that everyone looked towards the window, stopping whatever they were doing. Roseanna hurried to the door. I rushed towards Margaret and she held me, her arms tight around me. Then she led me outside to the car.

There was no time to be afraid. I was put into the car, a black Ford, and before I could say 'Barnacullia', it took off down the steep hill to the main Sandyford road. I was in a world of my own now and I was going to somewhere unknown. I remember as the car passed Lamb Doyle's shop I felt it didn't matter where I was going, really. You see, I could do nothing about it, so I just sat there. I did not ask the two men in the front of the car any questions, nor did they ask me any, except if I was okay back there.

Then the car came to a sudden stop and we got out. I can just vaguely recall standing in the courtroom of the courthouse in Dundrum, and being asked my name by the judge. 'Patrick Touher, sir,' I replied. There were many people in the court. I remember the judge asking some men, 'Is there no other place we can send our friend Patrick to?' A Garda gave me a bar of chocolate and brought me outside and told me to play awhile. There were several older boys outside playing, and one of them asked me why I was there and I replied that I was being taken to get my tonsils out. The boy laughed and said, 'This is no hospital. These are cops, you know.' Just then a Garda came out and brought me into the courtroom. A little while later I heard my name being called out. A Garda came to me and brought me before the judge. The judge said, 'Well now, Patrick, it is the decision of this court to send you to Artane, as I can find no other suitable place for you.'

I said, 'Is that where I have to get my tonsils out?' I heard people laugh. Then the judge said, 'Well, yes, my boy. That's it. Yes, they'll get them out for you.' I can still recall the judge saying to the men sitting at the bench in front of him. 'For how long will Patrick be in Artane? How long will it take to find a place for him?'

'Six weeks,' came the quick reply. The judge looked down at me then and said, 'Well now, six weeks is not a long time, Patrick, is it?' 'No, sir,' I replied.

It was probably normal practice at that time for children to be fostered in their first seven years only. I'm not really sure. In any case I was soon back in the car for what was to be a long drive across the city, to the place that was to change my whole life. That place was called Artane Industrial School.

Patrick Touher

Extract 2

Extract from
Forever England

It was my fourteenth birthday and as a treat my mother was going to take me out for a knife-and-fork tea and then to the playhouse to see a performance of *Dr Faustus*. I went straight from school, going up on the train from Crosby to Exchange Station to meet her under the clock in the booking hall. The moment I set eyes on her, saw her face beneath her hat brimmed with roses, I knew something was wrong. It seemed that all my life I had been waiting to be caught out at something, and now I had been, though what it was I couldn't tell. She was very quiet and severe, and she kept looking at me sideways in a funny calculating way as if she'd never seen me before, and little beads of terror rolled through my head.

I hardly tasted my tea. We had ham and chips and bread and butter and it might have all been made of cardboard. She kept clearing her throat as if to make some pronouncement but all she said were things like, 'Sit up straight' and 'Stop kicking the table'.

She didn't say anything coming out of the theatre nor walking up Stanley Street to the station, and the Devil went with us every step of the way. We sat in silence as the train rocked through the darkness, past Seaforth and Bootle and Blundellsands. I pressed my nose to the window and pretended to be looking out at the black sea, but I was watching her profile reflected in the glass, her eyes staring at me, her mouth turned down. Then she told me, half way between Hallroad and Hightown.

After breakfast she had put my gymslip into the wash and found a piece of paper in that fatal pocket. I had no defence. I had written down some verses of a naughty rhyme told to me by Rita Moody. I was good at art and I had illustrated them. My mother had rung up the school immediately and told the headmistress, who had asked her to come and see her that same afternoon. It was that important. I could infect the whole school, a rotten apple in the barrel.

When the train reached Formby my dog Pedro was waiting for me under the lamp on the corner by the council offices. He bounded towards me, and then, as if sensing my mother's disapproval, he slunk down and let me pass, not wanting to be contaminated.

We entered the house by the front door, which was peculiar; usually we went up the side path to the scullery to save the carpet in the hall. I went straight upstairs and hung about on the landing. It was freezing and I tried opening the airing-cupboard in the bathroom to get warm and some of the dahlia tubers fell out and rolled across the floor. My brother called out, 'Is that you, Beryl?' and I said, 'Yes, what do you want?' and he said, 'Nothing, nothing from you. You're beyond the pale.'

My parents weren't speaking downstairs and I didn't know if I could go to bed. I hadn't a room of my own and I wasn't sure if I'd be allowed in my mother's bed seeing I was so degenerate.

The next day I was in the gardens of the school with my best friend, rummaging in the flower beds for treasure, when Miss Johnson the biology teacher came up and said the headmistress wanted to talk to me. I'd only ever seen her before on the platform in prayers or in the corridor, and she seemed smaller face to face and much redder in complexion. She said that there were some things in life that were very beautiful and sacred and mustn't be trampled on. I thought she meant the flower beds and I said I hadn't stood on them, and she told me that I must make a great effort to cleanse my heart. I just sat there, looking at the papers on her desk; outside, I could hear my friends shrieking beneath the windows, pulling leaves from their bottoms as they played at having babies. When she had finished her chat the headmistress gave me a book about bees.

Beryl Bainbridge

Extract 3

Extract from

And None Of It Was Nonsense

I had a favourite book. It was filled with stories and puzzles and bits to colour in. There were just a few glossy pages, one of which portrayed three fairies, delicate with dragonfly wings, two of them tall, elegant wisps and the other rounded and little. My sister said she was the one with the raven hair, my cousin Brenda was the redheaded one and I was the baby fairy wearing no clothes. But I recognized this as a rather silly idea because I had always worn clothes and my father would never have allowed any of us to do otherwise: he didn't even like anyone to see his own bare feet, never mind letting me have a bare . . . anything except face, arms and legs.

The book came in for a good deal of pounding. The edges of the pages had become blotting-paper mushy and curly, while the spine had almost come adrift, making the threads of cotton underneath pickable. I was enormously fond of this book, and it was only on the most irritable of occasions that scribbles appeared on the duller pages in blue crayon; on happier days I would sit alone in my bedroom speaking aloud straight from the neat rows of little black letters where the tales were kept, in imitation of the voices my sister adopted when she mesmerized me with the activities of all the different characters involved – elf and ogre, dragon and princess, wicked stepmother and impoverished youngest son.

But what was most special about this book, making me keep it out of the way of prying eyes and thieving fingers, was not the contents so much as the cover. It was predominantly blue and red, presenting a pair of chubby children looking like the Ladybird boy and girl before the jeans era, who held between them a large book which they pored over with evident delight. On the cover of the book they were looking at were a pair of chubby children . . . and so on, the same pair of children with themselves on the cover doing what they were doing ad infinitum.

A magnifying glass, stronger than the one in the drawer under the pipe rack where my father kept the secret things I played with when he was at work, would reveal many, many more pairs of children reading my book. Of that much I was sure. But even a magnifying glass – or a telescope! – could not reveal all. The endlessness of it was endlessly a source of interest, food for thought. With bitten fingernail I traced the outline of as many books as I could see, and marvelled that an unimaginable number of smaller and smaller books continued beyond my physical and mental reach.

A day came, however, when this area of peace and privacy became public in terrible fashion. It had to do with school, as unpleasant things tended to do. It was a day when some kind of confusion attended the grownups' normal routine. The room partition was pulled back, children from other classes appeared and sat amongst us, and Miss Chilcott (our teacher, tall as a crane, as cold as her name, twin-setted and pearl-necklaced) was joined by Miss Smale. They consulted with each other for what seemed ages up front, presumably over what they were going to do with us.

Suddenly there was a look of purpose upon our teachers and they were shooshing us into silence. Miss Smale said we would have a story. There's lovely! We didn't have stories anything like often enough at school.

Well, we'd all have a story today. Our teachers were ready at last and Miss Smale was about to start. 'Once upon a time, in a deep forest . . . ' But I heard no more of that story. Miss Smale lifted the book from which she was reading so that the cover became visible to us. The cover was predominantly blue and red. On it was a picture of two children, a boy and a girl, looking like the Ladybird children, who held between them . . . It was not possible. But there it really was in Miss Smale's podgy hands: my favourite book. My mind, my thoughts, my secrets seemed to have ballooned together and burst into shapeless fragments. My favourite possession! How could such a gross intrusion have occurred! Miss Smale was too fat to have hidden in my bedroom. Somebody smaller must have got through the window and secreted herself (or himself! unthinkable! what would my father say?) under the bed. But when and for how long? Had the thief observed me pretending to be my reading sister or talking to myself at the window or exploring my private thoughts? Then she – someone – had stolen my book and a piece of my secret self.

My first tears were soundless, but as my incredulity turned to hysterical outrage, the noises I tried in vain to stifle increased well beyond the level that teachers can ignore. Everyone looked at me in amazement as they cried out superfluous appeals to our teacher on my behalf. I don't think I saw them. I certainly don't remember making the trip from my desk to the front of the class where in a blur I saw both those women bending over my weepings, howlings and hiccuppings, badgering me for the explanation of my startling piece of class disruption. I didn't want them to touch me, these thieves. I could only wail, my eyes screwed up but fixed upon what was lying on the teacher's desk while all other eyes were fixed on me. Miss Smale and Miss Chilcott cajoled, sighed, blotted my wet cheeks and tried to put their arms round me, but I shoved them off, the crooks, because I didn't want them between me and my book. 'What's the matter, Betty? What's the matter?' They asked the same question over and over.

Finally, my finger pointing hard, I hurled the words at them: 'That's my book!'

This no doubt cleared the air for them, but not for me. I could neither believe nor understand them when they talked to me about publishers and piles of books in bookshops and lots of other books being like mine. Nor could I understand why, after what I had told them, they wouldn't let me take my book home. But most remarkable of all was that later on when I went into my bedroom it had been put back exactly where I had left it. During the weeks that followed I lost interest in it – well, the goodie-goodies on the cover – and took up with a fat volume of Aesop's fables, lots of which I found I could read properly all by myself right to the very end, where there was always a moral to every story.

Betty Rosen

Activities

1 Copy and complete the following plot grid for the extract from *Fear of the Collar* (pages 69–71). The plot grid will help you to make sense of the events.

Patrick Touher was dressed in ....
by ....
because ....

↓

Patrick thought he was being sent to

....
because ....

↓

He was taken by car to

....
where some boys told him that
....

↓

The judge said that

....
and Patrick was sent to
....

2   Work with a partner. Make your own plot grid for
       one of the other extracts in this unit. Share your
       plot grid with another pair who have worked on a
       different extract.

3   Betty Rosen's favourite book was special because she
       enjoyed looking at the cover. Write an account of a
       favourite book you enjoyed when you were younger.
       Include details about the cover, illustrations and
       content. Say why this book was special for you.

4   The three pieces of writing in this unit are all
       autobiographies. An autobiography is the true story
       of the life of the writer. However, in order to make
       the story interesting, the author will often choose
       which details to include, and which to leave out.

       Write an autobiographical story of a true event that
       happened to you when you were younger; for
       example, it could be about something funny or
       frightening. Start by making a plan. In your plan
       include interesting points about events, places and
       the people who were involved. Leave out any
       details which are not vital to your story.

Drama Activity

Re-read the extract from *Forever England* (page 72). In
pairs, act out the telephone conversation between Beryl
Bainbridge's mother and the headmistress. How would
each character be feeling? Perhaps Beryl's mother
would be feeling embarrassed as well as concerned or
cross.

Section 6
Hard Times

The words 'hard times' probably conjure up different images in each of our minds. We will all have our own ideas of what they mean, probably influenced by our own experiences. Four of the following extracts give us a glimpse into the hardships experienced by other people. The fifth extract '"I'm Not Dead!" Insists Corpse' was written for children and has a very different approach to suffering and hardship.

Read the introductions and extracts which follow before working through the activities on pages 93–94.

Extracts 1 and 4: Story of a Slum (page 83) *and* Girls Liberated by British Gift of £117 (page 87)

These two articles are true accounts of the hardships faced by people living in other parts of the world.

Extract 2: 'I'm Not Dead!' Insists Corpse (page 84)

This 'newspaper article' is taken from a book written for children. The book aims to bring history alive by making it funny and interesting. In this extract, the writer imagines what it would be like to write a newspaper article about this poor woman who was declared officially dead, had newspapers been invented in medieval times.

Extract 3: Millions Face Starvation in North Korea (page 86)

This is an advertisement by the British Red Cross, asking for money to help the starving people of North Korea.

Extract 5: Robinson Crusoe Found – 2 February 1709 (page 89)

The novel *Robinson Crusoe* is very famous, but not many people know that the author, Daniel Defoe, based his character on a real person, Alexander Selkirk. In this diary extract, Woodes Rogers writes about his astonishing encounter with Selkirk.

Extract 1

STORY OF A SLUM

B. R. Salve is in his fifties. He is disabled, one arm severed just above the elbow. He tells once more how, when he was three, he fell from a high place on a wall and broke his arm and elbow. This, he says, was the time of British rule and there was no treatment available to poor people; so the arm had to be amputated.

He has worked for the Collectorate of the city for 19 years. His wife is still a domestic worker in Colaba, earning 200 rupees ($6) a month at three different houses. They have three daughters, all at school. His house is poor: the metal walls are corroded, so that the sun shines through, forming strange lacy patterns on the earth floor; beams of light illuminate air that is thick with dust. The house is detached from others, and the sun on the metal makes it stiflingly hot. On a stone platform in one corner food is prepared. A low concrete wall separates a small bathing area from the living space. There is a corrugated metal barrel and a zinc drum for bathing water; some smaller water vessels for drinking stand on a ledge. The family's clothes hang from nails in the wall. On a wooden shelf is a clock and a vase of dusty plastic flowers. A locked wooden trunk, once painted blue, nestles in the corner. A black-and-white television is showing a Sunday-afternoon Hindi film; a woven tray for sorting rice grains hangs on the wall. Mr Salve says: 'If I had good hands, do you think we would still be living like this?'

The New Internationalist

Extract 2

'I'M NOT DEAD!' INSISTS CORPSE

'Oh yes you are,' says priest.

Chantalle Lemon, a lace-maker from Flanders, was hopping mad when she learned yesterday that she was officially 'dead'.

The 23-year-old Assistant Darning Executive told us her story.

'I'd gone home to get a new **darning mushroom** when I suddenly fell asleep. After a little while I was awoken by a blanket being thrown over me. I stayed absolutely still because I thought it was a burglar, and I didn't want to disturb him in case he was violent. Then I felt myself being loaded on to a stretcher and carried out of the house.

'I was taken to a place

which was obviously a church. It smelled all musty, and there were people chanting in Latin. I stayed still out of respect until I realized they were reading prayers for the dead over me. At that I threw off the blanket and said, "Here! What's going on?"'

Castanets

'Imagine my astonishment when the priest gave me a pair of castanets.'

---

darning mushroom: a small, wooden object, shaped like a mushroom, placed beneath torn or frayed material which is then mended, or 'darned'

'"What's this for?" I asked. "Flamenco lessons?"

'"No," he said. "You've got leprosy. You're now officially dead and we're going to take you to a leper colony where you can live with other official corpses. Whenever you come near us ordinary people you must rattle your castanets. Oh yes. And here's a pair of gloves because we don't want you touching us."'

Not a spot

'Apparently someone had spotted a white spot on my hand, which is one of the first signs of leprosy. I pointed out that it was just a bit of lace fluff which had been caught between my fingers, but they took absolutely no notice.

'"Sic mortuus mundo, vivens iterum Deo," said the priest. Roughly translated this means: God thinks you're alive but we don't.

'Then he took me away to the leper colony. And that was that.'

Medical review

Chantalle is pressing for a review but nobody will come near her in case they catch the dreaded disease.

'Sadly there is no cure for leprosy and none of us wants to risk it,' said a medical spokesman.

The Medieval Messenger by Fergus Fleming

Extract 3

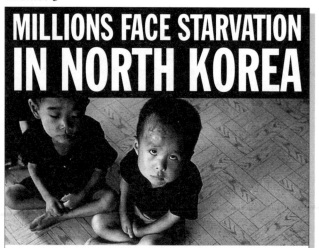

MILLIONS FACE STARVATION IN NORTH KOREA

This winter may prove to have devastating consequences for the people of North Korea. With the public's support, the Red Cross has ensured that basic medical and food aid has been reaching those who need it most. But supplies are running dangerously low at a time when help is needed more than ever before.

For the third consecutive year, a combination of devastating floods and drought has ruined harvests and destroyed homes. In parts of North Korea children are already having to live on a diet of tree bark and roots. But, without urgent help, many will not survive the bitter cold of the North Korean winter.

Help is needed urgently to avoid this catastrophe. In addition to food and medical equipment, blankets and winter jackets are now desperately needed. You can do something to prevent huge numbers of children suffering through the winter months. £26 could help feed a family of four for two months.

British Red Cross
Caring for people in crisis

Registered Charity No. 220949

Extract 4

Girls Liberated by British Gift of £117

Teresa Poole on how a little money, in the right hands, has transformed life for the water-carrying women of west China

ACROSS the arid mountainsides around Dabang village in the far west of China, fetching water is girls' work. Ma Fatima, a 13-year-old who is so shy she will barely talk, has for several years made three or four trips a day to fill her family's water buckets.

Until recently, each journey meant either a two-hour round trip to the river valley, or a hike to a dribbling spring at the top of a nearby hill where she would have to queue for her turn, often late into the night. Fatima, like most of the girls in the area, has never been spared from these labours to go to school.

The difficulty of obtaining water has blighted the lives of the girls and women in the mountain villages in this area for decades. 'In the past, girls from other villages did not want to marry into our village because there was no water,' said Ma Quanshan, a 32-year-old teacher. Even when the water was finally carried to the village, it was muddy and contaminated with animal excrement.

Two months ago all this changed for Dabang, the result of local people who decided something had to be done, and the donation of £117 from the little-known British Partnership Scheme. Not a penny was allowed near the local government officials down in the valley; nor did any expensive foreign consultants appear on the books.

The money paid for the materials and the skilled labour to construct a 'water-box', a utilitarian concrete container, over a previously buried natural spring. Every family sent someone to help, and this small amount of carefully-targeted money has transformed the life of the village. Inside the water-box is a permanent supply of hundreds of gallons of clean drinking water, just a 20-minute round-trip from Dabang. Teacher Ma's wife grinned: 'It saves me an hour and a half for each trip. At the top of the mountain we used to have to wait for a long time, but now the water is ready waiting for us.'

Independent on Sunday, September 1997

Extract 5

Robinson Crusoe Found, 2 February 1709

Selkirk, the real life Robinson Crusoe, was a shoemaker's son who ran away to sea and joined a band of **buccaneers**. *He was put ashore in September 1704 on the uninhabited Más a Tierra Island.*

Our **pinnace** return'd from the shore, and brought abundance of craw-fish with a man cloth'd in goat-skins, who look'd wilder than the first owners of them. He had been on the island four years and four months. His name was Alexander Selkirk.

'Twas he that made the fire last night when he saw our ships, which he judg'd to be English. During his stay here he saw several ships pass by but only two came in to anchor. As he went to view them he found them to be Spanish and retired from 'em, upon which they shot at him. Had they been French, he would have submitted, but chose to risque dying alone on the Iland, rather than fall into the hands of the Spaniards in these parts, because he **apprehended** they would murder him, or make a slave of him in the mines. The Spaniards had landed before he knew what they were, and they came so near him that he had much **ado** to escape: for they not only shot at him, but pursue'd him into the woods, where he climb'd to the top of a tree at the foot of which they made water, and kill'd several goats just by, but went off again without discovering him. He told us he was born at Largo in the county of Fife, Scotland, and was bred a sailor from his youth. The reason of his being left here

---

buccaneers: pirates/adventurers   **pinnace**: rowing boat
apprehended: understood   **ado**: trouble/fuss

was a **difference betwixt** him and his captain . . . He had with him his clothes and bedding, with a firelock, some powder, bullets, and tobacco, a hatchet, a knife, a kettle, a Bible, some practical pieces, and his mathematical instruments and books.

He provided for himself as well as he could; but for the first eight months had much ado to bear up against the terror of being left alone in such a desolate place. He built two huts with **piemento** trees, cover'd them with long grass, and lin'd them with the skins of goats which he killed with his gun as he wanted, so long as his powder lasted, he got fire by rubbing two sticks of piemento wood together upon his knee. At first he never eat anything till hunger **constrain'd** him, partly for grief, and partly for want of bread and salt; nor did he go to bed till he could watch no longer. The piemento wood, which burnt very clear, serv'd him both for firing and candle, and refresh'd him with its fragrant smell. He might have had fish enough, but could not eat 'em for want of salt, because they occasion'd a looseness; except Crawfish, which are there as large as lobsters and very good. These he sometimes boiled, and at other times broiled as he did his goats flesh, of which he made very good broth, for they are not so rank as ours; he kept an account of 500 that he kill'd while there, and caught as many more, which he marked on the ear and let go. When his powder fail'd he took them by speed of foot; he ran with wonderful swiftness thro the woods, and up the rocks and hills, as we perceiv'd when we employ'd him to catch goats for us. He told us that his agility in pursuing a goat had once like to have cost him his life; he pursue'd it with so much eagerness that he catch'd hold of it on the brink of a

---

difference betwixt: a quarrel between   **piemento**: a Spanish pepper with a red fruit   **constrain'd**: forced

precipice of which he was not aware, the bushes having
hid it from him so that he fell with the goat down the said
precipice a great height, and was so stun'd and bruised
with the fall that he narrowly escap'd with his life, and
when he came to his senses found the goat dead under
him. He lay there about 24 hours and was scarce able to
crawl to his hut which was about a mile distant, or to stir
abroad again in ten days. He came at last to relish his
meat well enough without salt or bread, and in the season
had plenty of good turnips which had been overspread
some acres of ground. He had enough of good cabbage
from the cabbage trees and season'd his meat with the
fruit of the piemento trees, which is the same as the
Jamaica pepper, and smells deliciously. He found there
also a black pepper called *Maragita*, which was very good
to expel wind, and against griping of the guts. He soon
wore out all his shoes and clothes by running thro the
woods; and at last, being forced to shift without them, his
feet became so hard that he ran everywhere without
annoyance, and it was some time before he could wear
shoes after we found him. He was at first much pester'd
with cats and rats, that had bred in great numbers from
some of each species which had got ashore from ships that
put in there to wood and water. The rats gnaw'd his feet
and clothes while asleep, which obliged him to cherish
the cats with his goats flesh; by which many of them
became so tame that they would lie about him in
hundreds, and soon deliver'd him from the rats.

He likewise tam'd some kids, and to divert himself
would now and then sing and dance with them and his
cats. When his clothes wore out he made himself a coat
and cap of goatskins, which he stitch'd together with
little thongs of the same that he cut with his knife. He

---

precipice: steep face of a cliff or mountain

had no other needle but a nail, and when his knife was wore to the back, he made others as well as he could of some iron hoops that were left ashore, which he beat thin and ground upon stones. Having some linen cloth by him, he sow'd himself shirts with a nail and stitch'd 'em with the **worsted** of his old stockings, which he pull'd out on purpose. He had his last shirt on when we found him in the island.

Woodes Rogers

The Faber Book of Reportage

---

worsted: woollen yarn

Activities

1 Re-read the article, 'Story of a Slum' (page 83).
   a Using the information from the text, draw a plan of Mr Salve's house. Mark and label all the objects in the room.
   b Write a comparison of Mr Salve's home and your own home.

2 Re-read the article '"I'm Not Dead!" Insists Corpse' on (pages 84–85). In pairs, discuss which parts of the article you think are true, and which parts are made up to make the reader laugh.

3 Look at the appeal for aid in North Korea on page 86. The appeal is effective because the writer has chosen his/her words carefully. Copy and complete the word wheel below with nouns and adjectives from the appeal.

Adjectives

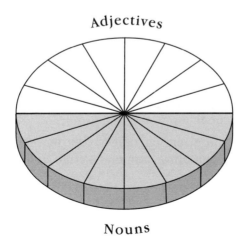

Nouns

4 Now look again at the article, 'Girls Liberated by British Gift of £117' (pages 87–88). Write your own appeal for donations for either the women of Dabang in China or the people living in the slums of India. Use some of the words from your word wheel.

5 **a** Work with a partner. Look back carefully at the diary extract 'Robinson Crusoe found' (pages 89–92) to find answers to the following questions:
   - What was Selkirk wearing when he was eventually rescued?
   - Why did Selkirk hide from the Spaniards?
   - Why was Selkirk left on the island?
   - While he was on the island, what did Selkirk eat?
   - How did Selkirk get rid of the rats?

   b Imagine that during his 4 years and 4 months of exile on the island, Alexander Selkirk was able to keep a diary. Write four diary entries, one for each year, showing how Selkirk coped with life on the island.

   c *Drama*
   Work in small groups. Make a sequence of frozen pictures entitled:

   - Left on the Island
   - Hiding from the Spaniards
   - Rescued!

   Now, at a given signal from your teacher, try moving smoothly from one picture to the next.

Section 7
First World War

The First World War (1914–1918) had a devastating effect on the lives of all those who were drawn into it. Casualties were appallingly high: over eight million soldiers were killed and twenty million were wounded. The extracts in this final section were all written by people who experienced the horrors of the war.

Look at the activities on pages 105–106 before reading the introductions and extracts which follow.

Extract 1: Letter from Wilfred Owen to his Mother
(page 96)

Wilfred Owen was a famous poet who died on 4 November 1918, just seven days before the war ended.

Extracts 2 and 4: A Nurse at the Russian Front
(page 98) and **I Was a German** (page 103)

These extracts give slightly different perspectives on the First World War. The first is taken from the diary of Florence Farmborough, describing her experiences as a nurse during the war, and the second is a German soldier's account of the misery of the trenches.

Extract 3: Letter from Ernest Hemingway to his Family
(page 101)

Ernest Hemingway survived the war and became a novelist. In this letter Hemingway describes his stay in the American Red Cross Hospital in Milan. Later, he wrote a book, *A Farewell to Arms*, which was based on his experiences in the hospital.

Extract 1

Letter from Wilfred Owen to his Mother

To Susan Owen

Tuesday, 16 January 1917
[2nd Manchester Regt, B.E.F.]

My own sweet Mother,

. . . I can see no excuse for deceiving you about these last 4 days. I have suffered seventh hell.

I have not been at the front.

I have been in front of it.

I held an advanced post, that is, a 'dug-out' in the middle of No Man's Land.

We had a march of 3 miles over shelled road then nearly 3 along a flooded trench. After that we came to where the trenches had been blown flat out and had to go over the top. It was of course dark, too dark, and the ground was not mud, not sloppy mud, but an octopus of sucking clay, 3, 4, and 5 feet deep, relieved only by craters full of water. Men have been known to drown in them. Many stuck in the mud & only got on by leaving their waders, equipment, and in some cases their clothes.

High explosives were dropping all around us, and machine-guns spluttered every few minutes. But it was so dark that even the German flares did not reveal us.

Three quarters dead, I mean each of us $\frac{3}{4}$ dead, we reached the dug-out, and relieved the wretches therein. I then had to go forth and find another dug-out for a still more advanced post where I left 18 bombers. I was responsible for other posts on the left but there was a junior officer in charge.

My dug-out held 25 men tight packed. Water filled it to a depth of 1 or 2 feet, leaving say 4 feet of air.

One entrance had been blown in & blocked.

So far, the other remained.

The Germans knew we were staying there and decided we shouldn't.

Those fifty hours were the agony of my happy life.

Every ten minutes on Sunday afternoon seemed an hour.

I nearly broke down and let myself drown in the water that was now slowly rising over my knees.

Towards 6 o'clock, when, I suppose, you would be going to church, the shelling grew less intense and less accurate: so that I was mercifully helped to do my duty and crawl, wade, climb and flounder over No Man's Land to visit my other post. It took me half an hour to move about 150 yards.

I was chiefly annoyed by our own machine-guns from behind. The seeng-seeng-seeng of the bullets reminded me of Mary's canary. On the whole I can support the canary better.

In the Platoon on my left the sentries over the dug-out were blown to nothing. One of these poor fellows was my first servant whom I rejected. If I had kept him he would have lived, for servants don't do Sentry Duty. I kept my own sentries half way down the stairs during the more terrific bombardment. In spite of this one lad was blown down and, I am afraid, blinded.

This was my only casualty.

The officer of the left Platoon has come out completely prostrated and is in hospital.

I am now as well, I suppose, as ever.

I allow myself to tell you all these things because I am never going back to this awful post. It is the worst the Manchesters have ever held; and we are going back for a rest.

I hear that the officer who relieved me left his 3 Lewis Guns behind when he came out. (He had only 24 hours in). He will be court-martialled.

Wilfred Owen Collected Letters

Extract 2

Florence Farmborough, A Nurse at the Russian Front

28 May [1916] Buchach

...We reached our quarters and prepared the bandaging-room without delay. Three or four wounded were brought before we were actually ready for them. We had bandaged those men and were busily engaged in unpacking our own necessary belongings and the first-aid equipment, when an urgent message reached us: 'Prepare for burnt soldiers.' Laconic wording, but elaborated in some detail by the staff messenger. A disastrous fire had gutted a wine-cellar; several soldiers had been burnt to death; some were being brought for instant treatment. It seems that the men of the 101st Permski Regiment had that day marched through Buchach, singing lustily, on their way into reserve. During the evening, several had gone on a tour of exploration. They found a distillery in which casks of alcohol were still stored. They drank their fill and then, inebriated and elated, turned on the taps. But someone must have struck a match, for the cellar was suddenly swept with fierce flames. About a dozen men perished on the spot; others crawled out, but collapsed and died soon afterwards. Only two of them were able to stand and they were brought to us.

They came, both of them, *walking*: two naked red figures! Their clothes had been burnt off their bodies. They stood side by side in the large barn which we had converted into a dressing-station, raw from head to foot. Injections were immediately ordered, but we could find no skin and had to put the needle straight into the flesh. Their arms were hanging stiffly at their sides and from the finger-tips of the men were suspended what looked like leather gloves; these we were told to cut off which we did with surgical scissors.

They were the skin of the hand and fingers which had peeled off and was hanging from the raw flesh of the finger-tips. Then we showered them with bicarbonate of soda and swathed their poor, burnt bodies with layers of cotton wool and surgical lint. We laid them down upon straw in an adjoining shed. In an hour or two, the cotton wool was completed saturated, but we could help them no further, save with oft-repeated injections of morphia which, we prayed, would deaden their sufferings. They died, both of them, before morning. And neither of them had spoken a single word! I don't think that anything which I had ever seen touched me so keenly.

Sunday, 31 July [1916] Monasterzhiska

Dinner was brought to us soon after our arrival. We sisters were still feeling affected by the awful sights which we had witnessed during that memorable journey. There was a heaviness within us difficult to throw off and although the menfolk of our contingent carried on a cheerful conversation we could take but little part in it. We had received instructions to delay the unpacking of all surgical equipment because we might have to continue the journey on the following day. We were still surrounded by gruesome remnants of the recent conflict. Not far from our tent, there was a slight incline with a couple of dug-outs; a dead man was lying near them, half-buried in the piled earth thrown up by a shell. Mamasha took a cloth and threw it over the discoloured face. To our right was a plain; there, too, was a litter of bombs, hand-grenades, cartridges, rifles, spades, pickaxes, gas-masks, shells exploded and unexploded. From where we stood, we could clearly espy the crumpled forms of dead soldiers. I took one or two photographs, but a feeling of shame assailed me – as though I were intruding on the tragic privacy of Death.

On another part of the plain, many bodies were

strewn; all in different attitudes – many on knees; others lying prone, with arms flung out; some had fallen head-first and buried their face in the soil; while still others were lying on their side, arms crossed as though they had found time to compose themselves before Death had released them from their sufferings. . . . It was a terrible battlefield; a sight which one could never erase from one's memory. There was another dreadful aspect – that of the ghastly smell of decaying human flesh. The sight of so many dead soldiers, left to decay in the hot sun and at the mercy of marauding flies, made a deep impression on us all. Our medical staff were highly indignant; they were taking the matter up immediately with the military authorities of the district and insisting that these forsaken bodies should be buried at once.

Farther away one could see long rows of devastated houses; another village laid desolate by our shells. God help the inhabitants! There was not one home left standing. It seems that some effort had been made to bury the dead, for to the north of that village a pit had been dug, in which some fifty soldiers had been deposited; the pit had not yet been filled in and here too the sight and smell of the decaying bodies were terrible. We left this gloomy halting-place and on the road, we passed a strikingly beautiful Austrian cemetery. The Austrians were particularly solicitous over their war-graves. This one was a neatly fenced-in plot with a rustic gateway, surmounted by a wooden cross and an inscription reading: *'Hier ruhen die für ihr Vaterland gefallenen Helden'* [Here rest the heroes fallen for their Fatherland]. Each grave bore a cross on which was inscribed the name of the soldier. Russian and German soldiers were buried there too. And a grave of a Jewish soldier bore a Star of David which the Austrians had scrupulously erected instead of a cross...

A Nurse at the Russian Front: A Diary 1914–18

Extract 3

Letter from Ernest Hemingway to his Family

21 July 1918, Milan

Dear Folks:

I suppose Brummy has written you all about my getting bunged up. So there isn't anything for me to say. I hope that the cable didn't worry you very much but Capt. Bates thought it was best that you hear from me first rather than the newspapers. You see I'm the first American wounded in Italy and I suppose the papers say something about it.

This is a peach of a hospital here and there are about 18 American nurses to take care of 4 patients. Everything is fine and I'm very comfortable and one of the best surgeons in Milan is looking after my wounds. There are a couple of pieces still in, one bullet in my knee that the X-Ray showed. The surgeon, very wisely, is after consultation, going to wait for the wound in my right knee to become healed cleanly before operating. The bullet will then be rather encysted and he will make a clean cut and go in under the side of the knee cap. By allowing it to be completely healed first he thus avoids any danger of infection and stiff knee. That is wise don't you think Dad? He will also remove a bullet from my right foot at the same time. He will probably operate in about a week as the wound is healing cleanly and there is no infection. I had two shots of anti tetanus immediately at the dressing station. All the other bullets and pieces of shell have been removed and all the wounds on my left leg are healing finely. My fingers are all cleared up and have the bandages off. There will be no permanent effects from any of the wounds as there are no bones shattered. Even in my knees. In both the left and right the bullets did not fracture the patella; one piece of shell about the size of a Tinker's roller bearing was in my left knee but it has been removed and the knee now moves perfectly and the wound is nearly healed. In the right knee the bullet went under the knee cap from the left side and didn't smash it a bit. By the time you get this letter the surgeon will have operated and it will be all healed, and I hope to be back driving in the mountains by the latter part of August. I have some fine photographs of the Piave and many other interesting pictures. Also a wonderful lot of souvenirs. I was all through the big battle and have Austrian carbines and ammunition, German and Austrian medals, officer's automatic pistols, Boche helmets, about a dozen Bayonets, star shell pistols and knives and almost everything you can think of. The only limit to the amount of souvenirs I could have is what I could carry for there were so many dead Austrians and prisoners the ground was almost black with them. It was a great victory and showed the world what wonderful fighters the Italians are.

I'll tell you all about everything when I get home for Christmas. It is awfully hot here now. I receive your letters regularly. Give my love to everybody and lots to all of you.

Ernie

Ernest Hemingway, Selected Letters 1917–1961

Extract 4

I Was a German

A devastated wood; miserable words. A tree is like a human being. The sun shines on it. It has roots, and the roots thrust down into the earth; the rain waters it, and the wind stirs its branches. It grows, and it dies. And we know little about its growth and still less about its death. It bows to the autumn gales, but it is not death that comes then; only the reviving sleep of winter.

A forest is like a people. A devastated forest is like a massacred people. The limbless trunks stare blankly at the day; even merciful night cannot veil them; even the wind is cold and alien.

Through one of those devastated woods which crept like a fester across Europe ran the French and German trenches. We lay so close to one another that if we had stuck our heads over the parapet we could have talked to each other without raising our voices.

We slept huddled together in sodden dug-outs, where the water trickled down the walls and the rats gnawed at our bread, and our sleep was troubled with dreams of home and war. One day there would be ten of us, the next only eight. We did not bury our dead. We pushed them into the little niches in the wall of the trench cut as resting places for ourselves. When I went slipping and slithering down the trench, with my head bent low, I did not know whether the men I passed were dead or alive; in that place the dead and the living had the same yellow-grey faces.

Not that we always had to find a dumping place for the dead.

Often the bodies were blown to pieces, so that only a shred of flesh sticking to a tree stump told where a man had died.

Or they rotted away in the barbed wire between the trenches.

Or if a mine blew up a section of the trench the earth was its own grave-digger.

Three hundred yards to the right of us, in that witches' cauldron, was a blockhouse which had been occupied twenty times by the Germans and twenty times by the French. The bodies of the dead soldiers were heaped together in one vast embrace. An appalling stench hung over them and they had been covered with a thin layer of white quicklime.

I was at the front for thirteen months, and by the end of that time the sharpest perceptions had become dulled, the greatest words mean. The war had become an everyday affair; life in the line a matter of routine; instead of heroes there were only victims; conscripts instead of volunteers; life had become hell, death a bagatelle; we were all of us cogs in a great machine which sometimes rolled forward, nobody knew where, sometimes backwards, nobody knew why. We had lost our enthusiasm, our courage, the very sense of our identity; there was no rhyme or reason in all this slaughtering and devastation; pain itself had lost its meaning; the earth was a barren waste.

We used to hack away the copper guiding-rings of unexploded shells out of sheer perversity; only the other day one had exploded and blown up two men – but what did that matter?

I applied for a transfer to the Air Force, not from any heroic motive, or for love of adventure, but simply to get away from the mass, from mass-living and mass-dying.

But before my transfer came through I fell ill. Heart and stomach both broke down, and I was sent back to hospital in Strasbourg. In a quiet Franciscan monastery kind and silent monks looked after me. After many weeks I was discharged. Unfit for further service.

Ernst Toller (translated from *Eine Jugend in Deutschland*)

Activities

1 Before reading the extracts in this section, make a note of anything you think you already know about the First World War. Work with a partner, and then share and compare your ideas with the rest of the class.

2 Now read the texts and try to build up a picture in your mind of life at the front during the First World War. Make a table like the one below. Use the first column to note any events and descriptions which you find very memorable. Use the third column to quote from the texts by copying any striking words or word clusters.

Life at the front	Writer	Key words or phrases
Wet conditions in trenches	Toller Owen	
Unburied dead	Hemingway Farmborough Toller →	'yellow-grey faces'

3 Now use your notes from the table to either:
   a Write a factual account of life at the front
   or
   b Write a poem in which you imagine you are a soldier in the First World War about to go into battle.

4 Re-read Florence Farmborough's diary entries (pages 98–100) and make a table like the one on the next page.

a Look back carefully at the diary entry for
28 May. Find, and note on your table, all the
adjectives which Florence Farmborough uses to
describe the nouns which are printed in the first
column.

NOUNS	ADJECTIVES	VERBS
message		gutted
soldiers		
fire		
flames		
figures	naked/red	
flesh		
bodies		
injection		

b Now complete the third column. In this passage
the writer has chosen to use some very powerful
verbs, for example, 'gutted'. Find seven more
verbs which you feel convey the tragedy of the
incident.

5 Imagine you are a patient in the hospital. Write a
letter to a friend describing what happened on
28 May 1916. Use the words from the table to help
you.

Acknowledgements

The editor and publisher would like to thank the following for permission to use photographs/copyright material:

BBC Worldwide for 'How I Created ... Paddington Bear' from 13–19 September 1997 issue of *Radio Times*, pp3–4; 'The Spying Game' and 'Letter to the Editor' from July 1997 edition of *Books for Keeps*, pp5, 13–14; BBC Worldwide for 'Gillian Cross, Author', from *Treasure Islands 2* by Michael Rosen & Jill Burridge, BBC Books 1993, pp9–12; 'Chopped Charlie's Last Chance' and 'The Terror of Tedworth'. Text © Terry Deary, 1996, Illustrations © Martin Brown, 1996, first published by Scholastic Ltd, pp19–21; The Dovecote Press for 'Haunted by a Fiddler' from *East Anglian Curiosities* by Rick O'Brien, p22; LCD Publishing for 'Haunted Britain – The Real X-Files' from *Unexplained Beyond Reality*, p23; Robert Hale Ltd for 'The Walberswick Whisperers' from *The Supernatural Coast* by Peter Haining, pp24–25; Illustrations and text taken from *How to Look After Your Rabbit* © 1995 Colin Hawkins. Reproduced by permission of Walker Books Ltd, London, pp31–34; John Murray Publishers Ltd for 'Pets' from *An A–Z Guide to Fatherhood Goodies and Daddies* by Michael Rosen, p35; BBC Wildlife Magazine for the advert on p36; Born Free Foundation for 'Fly Away Home', pp37–41. For details of membership to Born Free call 01306 712091; the extract on pages 42–43 from *The Aye-Aye and I*, reproduced with permission of Curtis Brown Ltd, London on behalf of The Estate of Gerald Durrell. Copyright Gerald Durrell 1992; International Rail for 'The Ride of Your Life', pp51–53; The O'Brien Press for the extracts on pages 69–71 from *Fear of the Collar* by Patrick Touher; John Johnson for the extracts on pages 72–74 from *Forever England* by Beryl Bainbridge; ''I'm Not Dead!' Insists Corpse', reproduced from *Medieval Messenger* by permission of Usborne Publishing © 1996 Usborne Publishing Ltd, pp85–86; The British Red Cross for the advert on p87; *The Independent* for 'Girls Liberated by British Gift of £117' by Teresa Poole, pp 88–89; the letter on pages 98–99 taken from *Wilfred Owen: Collected Letters* ed. Harold Owen and John Bell. © Oxford University Press 1967, pp427–428, by permission of Oxford University Press; Constable Publishers for the extracts on pages 100–102, from *A Nurse at the Russian Front: A Diary 1914–18* by Florence Farmborough; HarperCollins Publishers for the letter on pages 103–104 from Ernest Hemingway to his Family, taken from *Ernest Hemingway, Selected Letters 1917–1961*, ed. Carlos Baker.

Photographs
Hutchison Library, p51; J. Allan Cash Ltd, p52; Bridgeman Art Library/British Library, p85; Michael Bond c/o The Agency for the photo and illustration, p3.

Room 13

By Robert Swindells

There had been no number on the door. She knew there hadn't, yet there it was. Thirteen. And somebody was in there. Somebody, or something . . .

The terrible nightmare Fliss has before the school trip to Whitby is becoming a chilling reality. The hotel they are staying in holds a sinister secret. Every night at the stroke of midnight something strange happens to the cupboard on the hotel's dark landing. None of the teachers will believe what Fliss has seen but time is rapidly running out for Ellie-May Sunderland. Fliss will need to act quickly if she is to be saved . . .

Winner of the Children's Book Award

Age 10+   ISBN: 0 435 12499 4

The Last Vampire

By Willis Hall

Holidays are meant to be relaxing . . .
aren't they?

•

When the Hollins family decide to go
abroad for their holiday, they have no
idea what lies in store for them.

Losing their way in a dark and
mysterious forest, they set up camp at
the foot of an ancient castle. As the night
sets in, Henry begins to feel uneasy. The
howling he can hear from the forest is
definitely not made by dogs and he
knows that there is something weird
about the castle. When he sets out to
investigate the castle, he makes a
discovery which is even stranger than
anything he had imagined . . .

Age 10+   ISBN: 0 435 12488 9